MW01616063

Dog ¦

Learn dog parkour through games-based training you can play anywhere with your dog.

Play away your dog's fears and anxieties with games that strengthen its self-confidence, body awareness and trust in you and its environment!

By Anna Louise Kjaer

Dog Trainer and founder of 4-Paws Canine Academy
www.4pawscanineacademy.com

Studying for a Bachelor of science honour degree in animal behaviour at University of Aberdeen

Pro Dog Trainer certified by absoluteDogs Ltd (2018)

Dog Training Instructor of Denmark's Civil Dog Handlers' Organisation (DCH) - (2012)

I would like to thank all of the wonderful dog owners who contributed some lovely pictures of their beautiful dogs for this book!

They are all listed below in the order they appear in the book.
Black Spitz, Aske - My own dog
Working Cocker Spaniel, Belle - Owned by Irene
Shetland Sheepdog, Callie - Owned by Karen
Australian Working Kelpie, Sirius - My own dog
German Shepherd, Asti - Owned by Susan
Standard Poodles, Ella and Cobbs - Owned by Gill
Border Collie, Fynn - Owned by Sue
Jack Russel Terrier, Ming - Owned by Birthe

This book is dedicated to all of my wonderful students who keep coming back for more both from Denmark and Scotland. It is dedicated to my wonderful Grandmother for always supporting me and always having been ready to act as a "Limousine service" if I needed to go somewhere before I could drive. The book is also dedicated to my mother and father who got me interested in dogs from a very young age. It is also dedicated to my boyfriend who has been patiently supporting me from the side-lines and even took some of the great pictures for this book - but, the book is first and foremost dedicated to my first dog, Aske, who taught me how to train dogs and taught me to keep believing in them despite them not always listening. He taught me everything I know about dogs. Thank you Aske. I hope you are proud of me and looking down on me from the heavens.

-You train me and I train you-

Contents

4-Paws
CANINE ACADEMY

Basic Dog Parkour Games
Start out simple by playing the games that make up the foundation of the dog parkour sport.

Environments
Once you have gotten some of the basic games down, try to spice up your training by playing these games in new, fun, and challenging environments.

Puppy Parkour Games
Is your dog not quite old enough yet to do jumps or other more physically demanding exercises? Try some of these activities with your puppy while it grows.

Advanced Dog Parkour Games
Feeling ready for something more challenging? Have a look here for ideas on how to advance the basic dog parkour games.

My background

When I was born, I was brought home to a family with two dogs. I was put on the floor on a blanket with no protective barriers around me. The two dogs were let into the room and immediately they started sniffing the weird looking creature lying on the floor. Despite both of them being very excited and energetic dogs when welcoming the family home, they did me no harm while I lay there on the floor. They were licking me all over, gently pushing me with their noses to try and turn me over and caressing me with their tongues and noses. Since then they became my best friends growing up, and they always looked out for me.

My mother was a dog handler at the time and shortly after became a certified dog training instructor in one of Denmark's major dog training organisations at the time. I was brought to the dog training club the first time when I was only about a week old, and I was brought there every week ever since. I practically grew up in a dog training society. From as soon as I could understand general speech, I was taught to respect the dogs, never go to them if they were sleeping in their beds, never touch their food, and never pull their tails. Later I was taught how to read a dog's body language across many different breeds.

My father was training search and rescue with our oldest dog, and I admired how the dog could stay committed when tracking a man for several miles, I admired his focus towards my father, and I admired his courage and trust in my father. That dog was my idol and he was the reason why I at a young age decided I wanted to spend the rest of my life with dogs.

Like any other child, I wanted my own dog. I didn't just want a puppy, I wanted a dog. I understood that it meant having the dog for the rest of its life and that I would have to put the dog first and have to say no to many other things such as playing with friends right after school. I had to take care of the family's oldest dog for 2 years to prove that I was ready to handle getting my own dog. That meant I had to walk him, pick up his poo, feed him and train him at the dogtraining club every week and remember to train at home to be ready for the next week. I was also given dozens of books to read about dog training, dog behaviour, puppies, young dogs, how to choose the right puppy, how to avoid problem behaviours, etc. I did all this, and I loved doing it. I never complained.

When I turned 10 years old I had finally proven that I was committed and that I knew what it meant to have a dog and to take care of it. A month later my puppy was born. I was so lucky that the breeder agreed to meet me despite my young age, and I was even more lucky that she decided that I was good enough for one of her pups. I was even put before other people on the waiting list. I assume she must have seen how committed I was and how good I already was with dogs. I met my dog for the first time shortly after he opened his eyes. I had of course fallen in love with one of the two males in the litter long before I had observed any development. But luck was with me again, and it turned out that I had chosen the best puppy that I could have ever wished for.

Soon we started training at our local dog training club. We loved training and we always practised at home. Aside from all the general obedience we had to learn, I also experimented with many different tricks. I had never seen many dog tricks before, and certainly never had explained to me how to teach any of them to your dog. I figured all this out on my own by simply doing trial-and-error with my dog. We quickly developed a very strong relationship and he learned many tricks from a very young age. We impressed many people at our dog training club – especially due to my young age, I think. Back then, people did not really train tricks anywhere, and no one in Denmark knew anything about dogdancing either. It must all have seemed very out-of-the-blue with our many different tricks. In 2011 I was asked by my dogtraining club if I wanted to become an instructor. I said yes, and soon I was doing the instructor education in Denmark's Civil Dog Handlers' organisation (DCH). I was fully certified with a speciality in agility in 2012, only being 14 Years old. I was at the time, Denmark's youngest fully-educated and certified dog training instructor.

We competed a lot, me and my dog, in both local and regional competitions - mostly in agility. We also did some rally obedience, but my dog preferred agility at the time. After several years, dog dancing finally became known in Denmark amongst the different dog training circles, and of course we had to compete in this as well. We started out with skill tests which simply tested your dog's ability to do different cool tricks which were often used in dog dancing.

Alongside our many on-going ambitions within various dog sports, we also used every opportunity we got to train. This is where we learned to utilise the environment we were in and only our own imaginations set a limit to what we could do. This was one of our true passions as it was not about rules or competing against other people. This was simply enjoying working with each other wherever we were and challenging ourselves on our own terms. We could use as many treats as we wanted to and we could do whatever we wanted to. This was PURE fun. With no expectations. We later discovered that someone called this "dog parkour".

Dog parkour went from something we were doing when we didn't know what else to do, to something that was used at the pet shelter I volunteered at to boost the confidence of the dogs living there. This is where I truly understood the wonders of this sport and the potential it had.

Now I'm studying at the University of Aberdeen for a bachelor honours degree in Animal Behaviour where I also study the anatomy of different animals along with their many different muscles and how they work. This is a big interest of mine, and I believe dog parkour will in the future be used much more often in relation to building confidence in dogs as well as in rehabilitation after injuries. This is not just a fun sport - it is also an immensely useful tool which you can use to better your dog's life.

I hope you will enjoy this journey as much as I have.

What dog parkour *is*

When people first hear the words "dog parkour" I am sure most of them will have seen the human version of parkour and therefore, with the safety and welfare of the dog in mind, become naturally biased against the dog sport. "What good would come of teaching a dog to do a backflip or literally running on walls?" or "It's cruel to train a dog to jump from rooftop to rooftop in case it falls down, which it surely will at some point!"

-Actually, I couldn't agree more with the above statements.. – if they were true about the sport, that is.

Luckily, dog parkour is not as insane as the human version, despite there being several videos on YouTube of a dog performing incredible and sometimes insane parkour exercises next to its owner. However, for the majority of the dog training society, dog parkour is actually all about safety, control, and fun on the dog's own terms.

Dog parkour is simply put the performance of obedience on top of, underneath, or between certain obstacles. Your dog only needs to know the most basic commands from general obedience to be able to perform dog parkour. What makes dog parkour different from general obedience or more advanced tricks training is how you use your environment and incorporate it into your training. Teaching your dog to interact with its nearby environment can increase its own self-esteem as well as your mutual teamwork. As I will talk a little more about further on in the book, dog parkour will also decrease certain anxieties in dogs and prevent them from occurring through proper teambuilding and confidence boosts. The wonderful thing about dog parkour is that you can train this absolutely anywhere! So really, there is no excuse not to try.

Later on in this book I will take you through many different environments and show you how you can use them. I will also introduce you to many different tricks you can teach your dog which can be used to further challenge your dog or simply make what you are doing look super awesome, both at beginner level and advanced level.

But for starters, to give you the most general and basic idea of what dog parkour is, it all comes down to these 4 basic exercises: crawling under obstacles, walking around obstacles, jumping onto different platforms and balancing on different obstacles. These help give our dogs better motor skills and thereby help increase their overall physical abilities.

Benefits of training dog parkour

- You can greatly improve your dog's general and fine motor skills.
- It will improve your dog's confidence.
- Improve your dog's blood circulation.
- Any dog can do this
- It never gets boring and your dog will absolutely LOVE being with you

Improve your dog's general and fine motor skills.

By training dog parkour your dog will get to use all of its body in a new and different way. This will help your dog gain more control and awareness of its own body and how to use it (Helton, 2007). Often, dogs do not realise that they have a hind body, and they can therefore find it difficult to balance on different objects or walk backwards. Training dog parkour will greatly increase these skills. Increasing your dog's motor skills and physical awareness can also be handy in your everyday life. Your dog will become better at walking up and down stairs simply because it is more aware of how it places its paws. This can help prevent any unfortunate missteps. Also, how many times have you had a dog that was standing in your way? How many times have you asked it to back away or move, and despite it trying, it moves rather clumsily or slowly? Dog parkour can help your dog get this extra sense of its surroundings and how to easily navigate (even backwards!) in order to give you more space.

It will improve your dog's confidence.

By asking your dog to perform different known tricks in new ways, or on top of different objects it will often at first seem challenging to your dog. When you help your dog to overcome this new challenge, your dog will become proud of itself and trust both itself and you more. By giving your dog a regular confidence boost you can help decrease and prevent certain anxieties. Anxieties are often caused by insecurities which is why boosting their confidence and self-esteem can help reduce the anxieties the dog otherwise experiences. By furthermore improving the relationship between the two of you, you also get a dog that trusts you more in different situations. This will help your dog relax.

Improve the blood circulation in your dog

By having your dog use its muscles in new and different ways, you not only build up more muscle mass and improve mobility, but you also improve your dog's blood circulation through the entire body (Heaton et al, 1978).

Any dog can do this

Despite dog parkour being a very physical dog sport, it is extremely customisable and can be structured to suit any dog of any breed, age, or physical abilities. You might have a puppy at home, which still needs lots of rest to develop properly, and has very fragile joints which you need to be aware of and careful with, but you can still start out with using platforms that are the same height as the dog's ankles, and you can use natural obstacles like uneven terrain in forests. I have devoted a chapter later on in this book to demonstrate some simple puppy dog parkour.

You might also have a dog with limited mobility due to an old injury or age. As long as the dog is not in pain, you can structure your training to suit its abilities and to limit strain on certain body parts. You can also use properly structured dog parkour exercises as rehabilitation exercises, however, you should consult with your vet or physiotherapy specialist first.

Guaranteed fun with your dog

When you become more experienced in incorporating your environment into your training and spotting potential dog parkour "props", you will never have to have two identical training sessions again. Your training will become so varied that you will never feel bored again, and most importantly, neither will your dog. Doing something new and different with your dog everyday will make you so much more interesting in their eyes, as it is never the same you are doing together. This keeps excitement high, and every time you prepare for training dog parkour, your dog will be getting ready for a new adventure. In dog parkour only your own fantasy and imagination limits your creativity and training. So bring an open mind every time you go for a walk with your dog and let the inspiration flow and grow.

Become your dog's #1 priority

Dog parkour is basically just like playing games with your dog. The constant variability, the exercising which releases adrenaline and endorphins, the closeness and teamwork you use and develop – it all adds into this bank account of good and positive experiences with you (Mitchell, 2017), and as this bank account grows, the more contact your dog will seek from you because YOU are the source of all the fun

> *"It takes approximately 400 repetitions to create a new synapse in the brain - unless it is done with PLAY in which case it takes between 10 and 20 repetitions." -Dr. Karyn Purvis*

and of all the payments that go into this account. This is also why dog parkour is a great tool for getting a dog that never pulls on the lead or shows great impulse control in new and distracting environments. Training dog parkour will promote the focus onto you and it will become much easier to build a strong relationship with your dog.

Proper praising

Reinforcement is the key to getting a dog to repeat a behaviour we like. Reinforcement can also lead to repetition of behaviours we don't like if we accidentally reinforce for that behaviour or if something in the environment reinforces the behaviour for the dog. This is why it is important to know exactly how the best way to praise your dog in different situations is. First, let's look at some different things that can be seen as reinforcers:

- Treats (obviously!)
- Toys
    - Sometimes simply just seeing the toy!
    - Chasing the toy
    - Playing tug of war with you and the toy
    - Holding the toy
- Verbal praise
- Playing with you
- Petting and touch
- Attention
- A good feeling
    - Feeling good while running away from you
    - Feeling good while chasing a squirrel
    - Feeling good by greeting other dogs or humans

Many, many different things can be seen as reinforcers for the dog, and in cases of continuous bad behaviour, attention or the environment has often been the reinforcer of that behaviour – even though the attention or interaction might not have been positive. But to a dog, negative attention is often better than no attention.

But let us focus more on what you SHOULD do when training dog parkour to reinforce your dog. Not only do you need to find the right kind of reinforcer, but you should also think about how you deliver the reinforcement. Different reinforcers and different ways of delivering them can be used to promote either higher energy or calmness in dogs. In dog parkour we want to promote calmness due to safety reasons. Therefore, it is preferable to use treats and to deliver them in a slow and calm manner. Verbal praise is also great, but not always sufficient if you want your dog to absolutely LOVE dog parkour. At least not in the beginning. Petting and touch can also be fine, but some dogs might find this uncomfortable, especially if they are balancing on something, and they might feel as if they are being pushed. Personally, I would not use toys either for praising in my dog parkour, because this will only get my dog super excited and this might cause him to fall down or simply become too energetic to maintain a relaxed posture. However, if I am not training dog parkour in any heights I can still use toys for rewards so if you feel that your dog would prefer a toy and is able to stay relaxed when getting the toy, then use that!

Whenever my dog has done something that I like, or want to encourage him to continue what he is doing, I will click or gently verbally praise him (depending on the wanted arousal level) and give him a treat. I will usually give it to him very slowly while also verbally praising him. A good idea is to make sure that you are only delivering one treat at a time so you don't accidentally drop some of them and cause your dog to jump after them or lose his balance trying to look for them.

Do not constantly walk around with treats in your hands or constantly lure your dog with treats in front of its face if it is balancing as this can cause your dog to lose focus of its own body, especially the hind part. In dog parkour we want them to become aware of all of their body, so if we are distracting them with delicious treats all the time it can cause a safety hazard and also prevent our dog from actively learning. This means that it can take much longer for your dog to actually figure out what you want it to do, and what you are praising it for.

Instead, have your treats in your pockets and with a calm voice praise your dog while you slowly reach for a treat in your pocket. Deliver the treat very slowly to your dog and make it easy for your dog to grab the treat so it won't have to reach out in order to get it. If your dog is on the ground, then feel free after having delivered a calm treat to give your dog a release cue and then give it its toy. A toy can be great to finish a session to make sure that the dog can think back and remember the nice play session at the end.

Bonus info: The primacy and recency effect *(Murdock, 1962)*

The primacy and recency effect are two concepts that describe memory. Simply put, the primacy effect explains how you remember the first parts of a sequence. Think of the following example: you are asked to remember a list of groceries. The list is only mentioned once and you will be rewarded for the amount of things you remember from the list, so you do your best to remember all of them. As the things on the list start to get mentioned, you repeat them in your head. In order to try and remember all the first ones, you repeat from the beginning each time a new thing is mentioned. As the list grows, it becomes harder and harder to remember all the new words, but you don't forget the first three or four items on the list. These items have through repetition integrated in your long-term memory. (Now, just a small notice. Long-term memory does not mean that you will be able to remember these for the rest of your life. But you may be able to recall the first couple of items from the list a couple of minutes after the exercise even though you haven't thought about them while having a break in between hearing them and recalling them). Being able to remember the first items on the list is described as the primacy effect. The recency effect, on the other hand, is when you at the end of the exercise is asked to list the things you remember, and you then still remember the last couple of items on the list. You remember these last items because they are the last items you heard, and they are still in your working memory. However, if you after a few minutes with a break in between was asked to list the items from the list, you would struggle more trying to remember the last items on the list. This is because you did not repeat these in your head as much, and after a while without thinking about these items they are lost from your working memory. This is the recency effect.

Believing that these concepts can also be applied to dogs and other animals we must assume that they will remember the first parts of our training session if we repeated some of the same tricks and exercises throughout the session, and for a little while they will also remember the last parts of the session. This can also be applied to feelings rather than specific tricks. This is why I always like to end each and every session by doing what the dog loves the most. It is a fact that we by nature remember negative facts and experiences better than positive, because we keep worrying about the negative and thereby integrate it into our long-term memory. So to ensure that our dog won't go home thinking this was really difficult we finish the session by doing something the dog with guarantee will think is fun.

Safety

Safety is very important when training dog parkour, and it can quickly become too easy to say "sure, my dog can get on top of that!" or "for a dog it is not that far a jump from that box to the other." In reality, however, there are many factors involved in performing successful jumps – or other activities for that matter. What is the surface like? Has it been raining? What about the lighting? May it be too bright for the dog looking in this direction? May it be too dark?

Make sure there is enough light!

You have to keep in mind, that a dog's vision is different from ours *(Miller & Murphy, 1995)*. A dog, for instance, has a hard time telling the difference between green and red colours. This is due to their dichromatic vision, where we as humans have a trichromatic vision. This basically means that we can perceive more different colours than dogs can. Colours do not just become black or white for a dog, however, it can become difficult to distinguish between certain colours. If there is then not enough light, it could even just be in the shadows, this distinction becomes much more difficult and a red object can simply disappear in a green background – being it a grass field or in a forest.

A dog will also become tired, or it can slip in the terrain, causing a certain activity to become unsuccessful. Therefore, if you are practising jumps or balancing on something above the ground, you should keep your dog in a well-fitted and comfortable harness so you would be able to catch it. A cheap harness from the local supermarket's pet section or a dog accessories stand at a pet show might not suffice as the dog needs to be comfortable in hanging with all its weight in this harness. Sharp edges or narrow bands can therefore hurt the dog if it were to fall. These harnesses might be great for your everyday use, but not for dog parkour. When looking for a good dog parkour harness make sure that the harness has wide bands and preferably some kind of padding inside. It should not restrict the dog's movements in any way either – so the famous Julius K9 harnesses would not be good for dog parkour as they restrict the movement of the dog's shoulders and legs.

Control is your best friend

If you want your dog parkour training session to be as successful as possible and minimise the chance of anything going wrong, you want to have control.

This means, that you should not just let your dog play around on its own on these obstacles. It also means, that is your dog extremely excited and hyperactive in its body movements you should avoid dog parkour until it has fallen down a little. Train something else until your dog is more relaxed.

Treats can both be very helpful – but can also be a hazard!

You need to be sure how your dog reacts when given treats and you need to know how to handle both treats and dog at the same time – remember, you might also be holding a leash with which you should be able to catch your dog in case it loses its balance!

You can use the treats as a reward when your dog has completed an exercise, to motivate it to move during an exercise, or to make your dog relax in a certain position. Do NOT keep the treats in front of the dog's nose all the time, as this might distract the dog from focusing on how to place its paws.

Equipment

Equipment

Let's go through the things you cannot live without when practising dog parkour and then the things you shouldn't live without when practising dog parkour.

Must-haves

There are certain things you most certainly cannot live without when practising dog parkour. The sole most important thing is AN OPEN MIND. Without this you will become bored after your first training session and you end up never actually challenging your dog and you won't overcome all these challenges and obstacles together which otherwise makes your bond so much stronger. Without an open mind you will not get a dog that BEGS you to train with him or her and go on adventures to find possible dog parkour spots. So with an open mind comes creativity, and then comes great and varied dog training, followed by a well stimulated and happy dog. You gain so much by just having the right mind-set.

Treats

Pick a reinforcer that truly means something to your dog, but can also be delivered and enjoyed calmly without leaving the current position. To me and my dog, at least, that would be treats! And loads of them! It is so much better to come home with extra unused treats which you can simply freeze or use the next day, than standing at the perfect dog parkour spot with your dog super focused and in the middle of having the best time with you, and then you realise that you've run out of treats. Poor doggie! So keep loads of treats with you when looking for dog parkour spots.

Love your harness!

You cannot practise dog parkour without a harness. Maybe as long as it is still the very basic exercises you only train on the ground or only at the ankles height it will be fine, but when you want your dog to go jumping up and down or balancing on different obstacles, you really ought to use one for your dog's safety. A single misstep while balancing only 40cm off the ground is enough to give your dog a very unpleasant experience. Even though your dog might have forgotten about this in a week, it will still have had that bad experience while being with you – and I wouldn't want a bad experience to be on my consciousness. So to prevent breaks of bones, trust or courage, get a good harness and wear it with pride! (or maybe let your dog wear it instead of you. Might fit better that way.)

Finding the perfect harness can be a bit tricky. It has to be very comfortable with good padding inside and wide bands. We don't want the dog putting its weight in the harness and then feeling narrow bands cutting into the skin. It should be strong and made to hold all the dog's weight. Of course we don't expect our dog to be hanging in the harness very often or for very long. Only a few split seconds until you have managed to get the dog up again or slowly put down onto the ground instead of falling and hurting something. Then it is also very important that the harness doesn't limit the dog's movement. Some harnesses limit the shoulder movement which can be very dangerous when performing sports and exercises that require full mobility of all muscles and joints. Aim for Y-shaped harnesses which have great support at the chest of the dog without any bands going across the shoulders. So when choosing your harness, make sure that there is great support at the chest and under the dog, while also checking that the shoulders are free.

Believe it or not, you don't actually need more than that in order to start training dog parkour. However, you don't actually need a knife to eat a steak, but it makes it much easier and much less messier. So now let's talk about what you SHOULD have.

Platforms!

We loove platforms, and they exist in many different shapes and heights, and they can be used for maaaany different things. When I talk about platforms, I don't just mean those fancy low ones that fit the length of your dog on one side and the width of your dog on the other. Mind you, it can easily be one of those, but it can also be so many other kinds. Anything that is stable and raised just a tiny bit from the ground is considered a platform. It could be a box of any kind, concrete steps, tables, chairs and [insert your own suggestion here]...

Paw pods!

My dog LOVES his paw pods, and they can be used for so many different things from precision work to balance exercises. I would not live without these, and they can often be found for cheap money in Flying Tiger Copenhagen (more and more shops are opening up internationally, so do have a search for your area!)

Balance (BOSU) Fitness balls!

Exercise and fitness balls are also great for dog parkour! If you place the big ball in a circular donut-shaped object such as a kid's swimming ring float so the ball cannot move, you can use the ball to practise your dog's balance. Ask them to get on top and practise going from stand to sit to lie down, alternating between the different exercises. You might also be able to find half-ball version of the fitness Ball so you won't need the donut!

Agility high jump!

The simple agility jumps that consist of only two poles in the ground and then a perpendicular pole going across joining the two side-poles are great for teaching many of the advanced dog parkour jumps as well! They can often be found cheap used or on Ebay.

Balance wobble boards!

Balance wobble boards are also great for improving your dog's balance and understanding of how their own body works.

Skateboards and rolling platforms!

Skateboards or other platforms with wheels can also be great fun and are great for teaching your dog to generalise their behaviours. If they can do the same tricks they normally do on the ground on something that moves a little whenever they move their body, then you're sure that they can do it almost anywhere.

Poles and lampposts!

Poles/Spears are great for teaching your dog to walk around an object without jumping on top of it. When the dog is confident in this exercise you will be able to generalise the behaviour and have your dog walk around any object you point to!

Hula hoops!

Hula hoops or car-tires. The hula hoop can be used for teaching your dog to run through different circular obstacles or to improve certain jumps, and the tires can be used in so many different ways which I will also introduce later on in the book.

The equipment above is really great when you want to teach your dog many of the basic movements which can be used in dog parkour or to teach calmness on objects before moving on to something bigger. They are also great if you find it difficult to find the super good dog parkour spots but still want to practise dog parkour at home as they can be used for almost anything – only your own imagination limits your creativity and training.

Using the above equipment on the ground before moving onto bigger obstacles will also strengthen your dog's muscles. This is a good thing to do before taking on "the world". Making sure that your dog is physically fit and able to perform the wanted exercises is very important, and while training and strengthening the muscles you also grow a more intimate bond with your dog as this is something you are doing together. Even though your dog might have perfect muscles it can still be a good idea to go back and practise these things as it can work as a great warm up or stretching after exercise.

The chapter photo was made by the very talented Kalina Zaton. You can find more of her work at www.kalina-zaton.blogspot.com

Basic Dog Parkour

Basic dog parkour

Let's start out with the very basics of dog parkour! First, we really just need to make our dog comfortable with our different obstacles and working on top of something. This basic training also strengthens the dog's muscles and makes the bond between you more intimate and stronger.

I have divided this section up into several games which your dog will love! You do not necessarily need to follow them in the order they are listed as all dogs learn differently and have different preferences. Some dogs might love getting on top of different objects while others prefer to walk around them, so it's entirely up to you to feel what your dog might prefer to do. Just remember to take it in the dog's own pace and if necessary – be patient!

With lots of treats and patience you will both love this sport of games very soon! Most of the following games will also have an expert level, but these will be introduced in the chapter about advanced dog parkour. If your dog masters one of the basic games, feel free to jump ahead and find the appropriate expert level game.

I'm The King Game

I'm The King Game

For this game you will need any kind of (in the beginning) low platform. The purpose of this game is for your dog to put its two front paws on top of the platform while still having its hind paws on the ground. Start out by simply placing your platform on the ground in front of you. Try to place the platform in between you and your dog, so your dog would have to step on the platform in order to get close to you. If your dog offers to do this straight away, praise your dog verbally and give your dog a treat while being on the platform. Wait for a few small seconds, and if the dog is still standing there, give some extra verbal praise and extra treats. Then give your dog a release cue (it could be "okay", "that'll do", "gettit", or whatever release cue you prefer), and throw the treat away from you.

Now, simply wait and see what the dog does after picking up the treat you just threw away. If the dog gets back onto the platform you praise it very much, give it some treats while standing on the platform, wait a few seconds and give it some more treats, and then release your dog and throw the treat away again. You can do this several times but make sure you keep your training sessions short so you do not end up boring your dog or making it so tired that it becomes frustrated easily. A good rule is you are allowed to repeat something 5 times before you should do something else. Then you can always return to the exercise later.

If your dog did not offer by itself to get back onto the platform, either try and wait a little longer and maybe move yourself around the object a little to ensure that the dog will still have to walk onto the platform in order to get to you, or try and lure your dog by throwing a few treats onto the platform. If the dog simply takes the treats without offering to get back up afterwards, try and keep the treats in your hand while luring it onto the platform. When it's back on top of the platform, praise the dog a lot and release it!

When your dog is offering to walk onto the platform every time, try and add a verbal cue while it is on its way back onto the platform after having run for the release-treat. Remember, later on we would like our dog to get all four paws on top of something, and in order for the dog to know the difference you should use two different verbal cues for those two behaviours.

When your dog is comfortable with the platform you have been using until now, you can try and change the platform to something else. This might confuse your dog a little, but that is okay. If your dog seems confused, you simply repeat the first steps again with this new object. Whenever the new platform is just as good as the first one, try and change to something new again. The more different things your dog learns to associate with this game, the more generalised the behaviour becomes. You can also try to use vertical structures such as walls or big bins at the streets. For the dog, this game will end up being about putting its two front paws on any object you point to. At some point you will be able to play "I'm the King" with anything as a platform! Some dogs learn this game super quick and others might take a while. Just remember to keep it fun and reinforce the behaviour that you want. The more you reinforce, the more often your dog will offer this behaviour.

The Time Game

The Time game

This game is about teaching your dog to walk around an object. I would start this game with an easy object such as a pole or some kind of spear which can stand by itself on or in the ground. I like to use pole-shaped objects here in the beginning to avoid confusing the dog. If you use a flat object the dog might see it as a platform and offer the wrong behaviour. To avoid this from happening and to avoid having to say no for an otherwise excellent platform exercise, I will simply just not make it possible for the dog to offer the wrong behaviour. It is quite limited what you can do with a pole-shaped object if you haven't been training tricks or dogdancing with your dog previously.

You can start this game in two ways depending on how your dog learns best; you can either shape it from the beginning or lure the dog until it gets a basic understanding of the game.

If you want to shape it, simply try and approach the pole with your dog and then slowly stop (not too sudden as this would draw your dog's attention to you rather than the pole) a few steps away from the pole. If your dog continues towards the pole even for just a single step, you praise verbally (or click if you prefer a clicker) and throw a treat either next to the pole (at 3 or 9 o'clock depending on which side of the pole your dog seems to be moving most towards) or behind the pole (everything from 10 to 2 o'clock, again depending on which side your dog is closest to).

Figure 1 - Demonstration of where to place the treat in relation to the location of the dog.

If your dog walks somewhat around the pole in order to get back to you, quickly praise your dog and throw a treat either right in front of the dog or preferably where you would want your dog to go next (further around in the circle). If your dog comes straight back to you, simply walk a little away with it and turn around and walk towards the pole again, repeating the steps above. If you feel like your dog is always returning straight to you, walk a little closer to the pole so you are able to throw treats in a circle around the pole. This is why I call it the Time game, as you should place your rewards around the pole alternating the position of the reward like following the time on a watch.

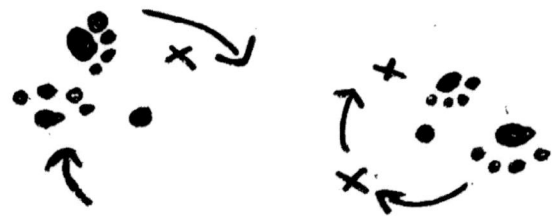

Figure 2 - Advancing the circle around the pole by throwing more treats in the direction you want your dog to go.

If you prefer to lure the basics of the behaviour, have a treat in your hand and simply lure your dog around the pole. Be aware, that dogs do have certain sides (left or right) that they prefer, just like people can be left or right handed. If you feel a little awkward, try the other way around the pole instead as it might be because you are forcing a "right-minded" dog to think like a "left-minded". Throw the treat at different stages around the pole alternating between the different hours of the watch. When this becomes a much easier and fluent motion, you can try and gradually face out your luring hand by lifting your hand a little higher, and slowly making your way from doing a full circle with your hand to doing a simple wave-like motion with your hand instead. Remember, when you are increasing the criteria or difficulty for the dog, you have to reinforce more often to prevent confusion.

When your dog becomes more fluent in this game and offers to go run around the pole you can add a verbal cue. When doing this, say the wanted verbal cue right before you ask your dog to circle the pole with whatever signals you used before; hand signals, leaning towards the pole, etc.

On Top Of The World Game

On Top Of The World Game

For this game we need some kind of platform again, preferably a wide platform to begin with and maybe a platform that is a little taller than the platform first used in the "I'm the King"-game to avoid confusion at first. The goal of this game is to get our dog's all four paws onto our platform. Again, you can try and do this in two different ways. Either by shaping or luring.

For shaping, place yourself behind the platform, so the platform is in between you and your dog. Wait for the dog to offer to climb onto the platform in order to get close to you. If it first offers only the two front paws, praise it anyway and simply place the treat further up on the platform, so the dog would either have to stretch far or climb further on top in order to reach the treat. If you are able to see the dog move its hind legs, praise for anything that looks like it is trying to use one of its hind paws to climb. Praise for every single small step towards the wanted behaviour.

If you want a more do-as-I-do approach, simply climb onto the platform yourself first (be sure that your platform can carry you and that you do not put yourself in any danger by climbing onto something). This can show the dog that it is possible to get on top of the platform, and that you want it all the way up. This is quite a fun approach, but if you haven't used this before, chances are that your dog might simply think you are silly. But feel free to give it a try!

If you want to lure this behaviour, simply show your dog that you have treats, and tap on the platform with your hand (if it's quite tall compared to the other platform), or simply drag the treat a little in front of the dog's nose until it jumps all the way on top of the platform. Again, praise for offering the two front paws, and then put a treat further onto the platform to try and lure the dog to climb further. If the platform is low, it will be quite simple and easy to lure it onto the platform – especially if the platform is also wide.

When the dog jumps onto the platform, praise it on the platform and then give your dog its release cue and throw a treat away from the platform (only if the platform is not too tall!). This will encourage the dog to try again without you telling it to go down, which is the opposite of what you want. If your dog does not offer to get back onto the platform, simply help it some more with the previous steps and reinforce it more.

Release it every time after having praised it on top of the platform to see when the dog understands what you want it to do. When it comes back onto the platform after having been released, add a verbal cue for the behaviour and use this every time the dog is on its way back from the release-treat.

Bum In The Air Game

Bum In The Air Game

For this game you would again need either a platform or a low stable fitness "pillow". The purpose of this game is to get our dog to stand with their hind paws on top of the platform and with their front paws on the ground. This helps strengthen their back and later on you can use it for stretching out the muscles in the hind legs or strengthening the muscles in the front legs and chest of the dog. For this game, I prefer to use a mix of shaping and luring techniques. For the simple level of this exercise, I always keep my platform perpendicular to my dog if the platform is long and slim to help ensure that my dog gets a success and don't accidentally step next to the platform instead of onto it. For the purpose of preparing you for the more advanced uses of this exercise, I am going to introduce you to how to get your dog to back up onto the platform rather than simply walking up and then down again.

To start this game, we want to give the dog the idea that we are working with the platform and we want a certain position on that platform. For this exercise we are going to backwards chain the behaviour. Backwards chaining means that while teaching the dog what to do, we start by showing it the end result and gradually add on more and more steps before the final result. Our goal behaviour is the dog standing with two hind paws on the platform and two front paws on the ground, so we start by luring the dog onto the platform and then a little bit further than the platform, so the dog ends up with its front paws on the ground. Give a few treats for standing like this with short pauses in between to let the dog realise how it is standing. Give it a release command and throw a treat behind the platform to allow the dog to seek back into the position itself. Once you've repeated these steps a couple of times, try to lure your dog even further down from the platform so it ends up with all its paws on the ground right in front of the platform. Here simply wait for the dog to offer to walk backwards, and then praise as soon as the dog touches the platform. If your dog is not good at offering behaviours, it might even be enough to praise for simply lifting one of its legs and "thinking" about maybe going to move backwards. At first the dog might get a little surprised when touching the platform while backing, but reinforce what it did with lots of verbal praise, a click, and if you can, give your dog a treat while it touches the platform with its hind legs. At first, do not wait for it to necessarily have both hind paws on the platform, but simply praise for a single paw. When this has been reinforced enough, the dog will become more confident in this game and later offer both paws due to excitement. When this happens you praise loads again!

Once you *know* your dog will attempt this behavior every single time, you can add in a verbal cue. Simply say the verbal cue you want associated with this behavior right before you expect your dog to start moving backwards. This way it will associate this new cue with the behaviour it is doing if it gets reinforced afterwards.

After a while, you can try to increase the distance between the dog and the platform slightly or use different platforms to generalise the behaviour!

Under The Bridge
Game

Under the bridge game

For this game, you do not necessarily need any equipment, but you can use anything the dog would be able to crawl under like a chair, a bench, a small table, etc. This game is basically about getting our dog to crawl under different things. In a forest it could be under a fallen tree stem or under the benches in the city. When teaching this behaviour for the first time I prefer not to use any equipment and simply use my own body instead. This allows me to get closer to my dog and actively be a part of my dog's game while helping it overcome the challenges together and thereby strengthening the bond between us. Depending on what you would like to get out of this behaviour, there are different ways of training it. For now, we are simply going to focus on getting your dog to crawl under obstacles, but if you would prefer to also have your dog being able to crawl out in the open without any obstacles, then jump ahead to the advanced section.

If you, as me, would prefer to just use your own body for this game, sit down on the ground with your legs bend to create an opposite V shape. Have your dog lie next to you and preferably looking through the V shape. For shapers, simply wait for your dog to either sniff in the opening or even move a little bit towards the opening. Praise them verbally and place a treat a little further ahead under your legs. Do this as many times at it takes for your dog to crawl the entire way under. Make sure, that before giving it a release cue after having finished, that your dog is lying down as to promote the closeness to the ground in this behavior.

For those who prefer to lure your dogs, start in the same position, and then with a treat in your hand, lure your dog all the way under your legs, praising it for even the smallest crawling steps. Don't worry too much if your dog tries to stand up when moving. Just stop any movement and wait for your dog to lie down on its own before giving the treat. However, do remember that they WILL need to lift a part of their body in order to crawl. They are dogs, not snakes. Here it is also important that you never give the treat while the dog might be standing up or doing a bow-like stand. Only give the treat when the dog is lying completely flat on the ground. Otherwise you might risk getting a dog that will go further and further up for every time you practice this challenge.

The Flying Game

The flying game

The flying game is often considered one of the most fun and engaging games. This is where all of our calm training is out-balanced by more excitement and speed. In the flying game, we want our dogs to jump over different objects. Some dogs might already be able to do this on their own or knows it from other dog-sports. But, if you are new to this game or if your dog does not know the game on command, remember to always start out low, no matter the size of your dog. It is also important to note, that if your dog is not at least 12 months old yet, you should not be practicing this game just yet.

For this I would use my pole again. By holding the pole in one hand, I can lure or encourage the dog to jump over the pole with my other hand. To make this easier for yourself, hold the pole in the hand that is closest to your dog, so you are able to lure further with the other hand. Otherwise your arm might not be long enough to fully lure your dog over the pole, or your arm might simply be in the way and confuse the dog.

Have your dog next to you in either a sit or a stand and walk a big step away from your dog to allow it some room for gathering speed and power enough to jump (even though the pole is only 5 or 10cm above the ground!). With the pole in the hand closest to your dog and a treat or a toy in the other, encourage the dog to jump over the pole. In the beginning it might just walk over the pole, but reinforce this behaviour anyway. As confidence in this behaviour grows, so does excitement and it might soon offer more power and then give a proper jump.

Other times, it CAN help raising the height of the pole a little bit since some dogs don't see the need for jumping when they feel they can just walk over the obstacle. Just remember not to do this too much as it can injure the dog if you are not careful – especially in the beginning of the training where the dog might not be as confident in the behaviour yet.

If you want to promote more excitement in the flying, try and throw the treat just as the dog is about to jump. This will turn on their hunting instinct and the dog will jump faster in order to reach the treat.

When your dog becomes more confident in this exercise, try and ask the dog to jump over your leg or your arm when sitting down. Slowly try and move on to different objects to jump over, but make sure that the object you are using cannot move, is not too tall, the terrain is somewhat even, and the object is not so wide that your dog might stumble on it when trying to jump over.

The Balance Game

The balance game

This game almost explains itself. Our goal is to have our dog balance on top of something. For the purpose of basic dog parkour, we only talk about having our dog walk on top of something such as the 30cm tall "walls" some people have separating the sidewalk from their garden, or walking on a single step on a wide staircase in the park. It could also simply be from one end of a bench to the other – anything that is raised slightly above the ground where the dog can walk for a shorter or longer distance.

This game is very much straight forward, especially if you already master the *"on top of the world"* game. One thing you have to be cautious about, though, is the height of the obstacle you want your dog to walk on as well as the material. Make sure that it is not slippery due to rain or mud, or that the obstacle suddenly increase in height. You should also make sure that you can control your dog while it is on top of an obstacle so your dog does not suddenly start running in a pace where you cannot follow and where it might fall down when it reaches the end of the leash. So keep the leash short so you would also be able to catch your dog in case it should slip. However, also be aware that you are not holding the leash too tight and thereby pulling your dog in any way. Try and find the right "balance" between when the leash is too long and too short.

Once your dog is comfortable being on top of different obstacles and walking along on longer platforms, you can have a look at the advanced dog parkour section for more challenges and inspiration to what you can do next. The advanced section will even include how to help your dog develop a sense of balance and build up a healthy amount of muscle mass. This requires great body awareness which the dog will also develop through some of the fun advanced games.

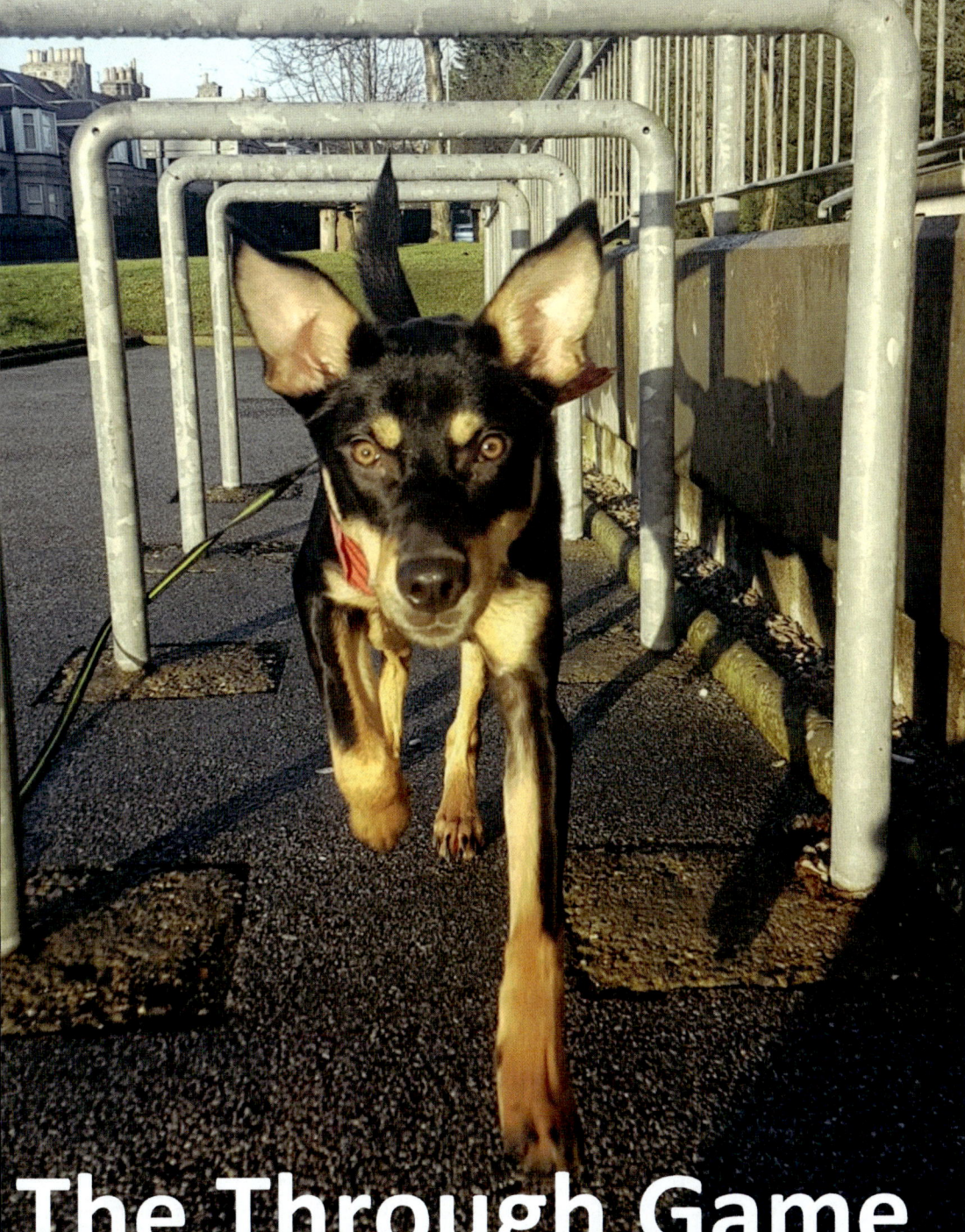

The Through Game

The through game

This game is super fun! When you play it out and about it almost feels as if you are running a sort of urban or alternative agility. What we want is to teach our dog to run through any kind of circular object like a hula hoop, a tire, certain bike stands, certain benches, or sometimes even a circular shape created by fallen tree roots. It is basically like seeing agility tunnels everywhere!

You can start practising this with either a hula hoop or a vertically standing tire (has to be prevented from falling when the dog walks through it!). Hold the hula hoop the same way that you would hold your pole in the flying game. Either wait for you dog to approach the hula hoop and praise for that, placing the treat nearer the hula hoop and eventually praising the dog for walking through it, or lure your dog with a treat in your hand. You can also, if the object (hula hoop or tire or whatever you are using) is fastened, so it can stand on its own, ask your dog to sit on one side of the object and looking through the hole, and then place yourself on the other side of the object and simply call your dog through. Some dogs might just walk around the object in the latter method, but if you want to stick with that method, you could have a helper that is gently holding the dog until it starts moving towards the hula hoop instead of seeking to walk around it. But be careful that the dog does not feel forced in any way to do anything it is not comfortable with. It will all come with time and patience and recurring training.

When you are giving your dog its release cue in this game, either throw the treat behind the hula hoop to get the dog back where it started, or throw it behind you and then move onto the other side of the hula hoop yourself. When your dog becomes more familiar with this game, you will no longer have to move and you can throw the release treat anywhere you want, and your dog will still seek back to run through your hula hoop.

Environments

Environments

As mentioned already quite a few times in this book, dog parkour can be practised anywhere and is one of the many wonders of this sport. It therefore does not matter whether you live in a big city, on the countryside or near a forest. However, if you feel like you have exhausted all the possibilities in your nearby environment, try to spice up your training by trying one of the other great environments. Below I will explain the three major dog parkour environments and come with suggestions as to what you can use in that particular environment. This is not, however, an exhaustive list and it is only your own imagination that limits your creativity and training.

The City

The city

The city has many potential dog parkour training obstacles when you have gotten used to looking for them and recognising them. It is just important that you remember to show respect for other people, as not everyone likes dogs and some might think you don't have control over your dog despite it being on a leash. Also, children's playgrounds can be wonderful dog parkour spots, but do not go there at times where other children might use the playground. Be aware, that even though you might have gotten to the playground before any children did, they still have more right to be there than your dog. Therefore, even though the children might not go directly to the playground, if you notice them somewhere else in the park, leave the playground so they won't have to feel uncomfortable approaching or asking for you to leave. Show respect.

Poles or bike stands can be used for the time game, or if they have been placed in a line next to each other you can have your dog walk slalom in between them. This is super fun and can be done in various speeds. If you want to really increase the difficulty, you can teach your dog to walk slalom without your help and maybe even on its own while you are waiting back at the beginning of the poles. Some bike stands might even be used for the through game. The through game can be combined with a simple slalom to make it look even more impressive and to increase the difficulty if your dog is super smart. Remember, by ensuring that you keep challenging your dog whenever something becomes too easy, you help mentally stimulate it because it has to use its brain and really think about what you are trying to ask it to do.

Any raised platforms are great for balance games or the more advanced stepping stone game. Steps can be used for I'm the king games, bum in the air games, on top of the world games, and balance games. You can also teach your dog to walk backwards up the stairs, use them to stretch or use them for simple balance games. Your dog can perform various tricks on top of the platforms, and if they are pillar shaped platforms, you can also trick your dog by asking it to play the time game instead of the on top of the world game.

Benches exist in so many different forms and shapes and they can be great for dog parkour purposes! Some benches have circular beams which you can use for through games or complex slalom games. You can also have your dog crawl under the benches, jump over them, balance on top of them, play bum in the air or use them as platforms for different tricks. If a bench has a backrest, try to come up with different ways you can incorporate the backrest into your games and training.

Playgrounds

As mentioned before, playgrounds can be great! However, be careful with all the different things that can move. We do not want to scare or injure our dogs in any way, and it is our responsibility to ensure the safety of our dogs while we train with them. Some playgrounds might have teeter totters which advanced dog parkour dogs can use for balance games. Ask your dog to slowly balance from one end to the other while the balance shifts in the teeter totter. When your dog reaches the middle, ask it to stand or stay in its current position. If your dog is advanced and used to teeters, simply ask it to walk slowly forward so the teeter will shift balance slowly without scaring the dog. If a moving teeter is new to your dog, ask it to stand nicely on the middle while you very slowly tip the teeter totter yourself, praising the dog for remaining calm on it. It can also be very helpful if you have a helper with you. Let the helper tip the teeter totter very carefully and very slowly while you stand with your dog and praise it while the balance shifts. Give it lots of treats, but be careful how you give them to your dog, so it does not feel the need to move in any way in order to reach the treats. If the teeter totter on the playground is very narrow, I would suggest practising the teeter from agility first, or any other teeter that might be a bit wider. This will make it less challenging and less frightening for the dog if it is its first time. If your dog is very confident, you can also simply try and practise many different balance games on narrow obstacles, so your dog gets used to balancing on something narrow before having to worry about the movement in the teeter as well.

Remember, dog parkour is all about giving your dog a positive and fun experience. We want to create a strong teamwork between you and your dog, and if your dog at any point feels let down because of a scary experience, this will affect your bond. Stay positive and take it slow. Be a good and reliable *teamplayer*!

There might also be small merry-go-rounds. These are great for both beginner and advanced dog parkour dogs. The beginners can sit nicely on the merry-go-round while you gently push it around. Remember to never push it hard while your dog is on! The pushing is only to help generalise the behaviour or trick you asked it to do on top of it. Being able to perform something confidently on top of something that moves is extremely incredible. It will also help make your dog good at generalising its behaviours and improve its own self-esteem by overcoming the challenge.

For advanced dogs you can evolve the I'm the king game by having them push the merry-go-round themselves with their hind paws on

the ground. If your dog is an expert you can play the bum in the air game while the dog pushes the merry-go-round with its front paws on the ground. If you want to go expert, you can also train your dog to know the names of each paw. With this you could ask your dog to use only one paw on the merry-go-round, and you could switch between all four paws. Dog parkour is not only about the dog being on top of things either. You could also teach your dog to push the merry-go-round with its nose. This looks super cute and is great for promoting calmness in more eager dogs.

Swing sets are way too often used by inexperienced dog handlers. I want to make it clear that I would never suggest anyone to place their dog in a swing (or any kind of situation that the dog cannot just walk away from if it is feeling uncomfortable!). I will not recommend getting your dog to jump over swings either, as there are so many things that could go wrong when doing so. But if you absolutely want to do it, please make sure that the swing cannot move while your dog is jumping over it. So have someone to hold the swing steady so the dog will not accidentally push it with one of its paws while jumping.

You can, however, teach your dog to push the swing either with a paw or with its nose. This is also great training and a great way of generalising different touch behaviours. If your dog is very experienced with slalom games, you can also evolve the slalom game into a more challenging game, where the obstacles do not have to be on the ground but can be in the air instead. Teaching your dog to walk slalom between swings hanging down is challenging, but great fun!

You can also use the beams for a variety of different games. You can do slalom games, I'm the king games, touch and target games, or if your dog is experienced, you can potentially do a bum in the air game on the beams. If they are narrow, practise somewhere else first and gradually train on objects that are more and more narrow. This will teach your dog even greater body control as it will slowly feel for something to put its hind paws on. Once it feels the narrow beam it will (when trained properly and with time) slowly and carefully place its other hind paw behind the other and walk slowly backwards onto the beam. This requires great precision, so this is not for beginners!

BMX Tracks

These are PERFECT for dog parkour! One would think they were designed as much for dogs as they were for bikes – but just as with the playgrounds, they are unfortunately not designed for dogs and we should respect its proper users. On BMX tracks there are often a great variety of different platforms or slopes. The slopes are great for generalising behaviour as well as practising the more advanced version of the bum in the air game where the dog is taught to walk backwards up on a vertical surface (only for adult dogs!). There might also be different kinds of railings which can be used for flying games or under the bridge games. At BMX tracks, your imagination can really run free and there is so much inspiration.

The Forest

The forest

Personally, I absolutely love dog parkour in the forest! There are so many things to do as well as fresh air and silence. When you yourself feel like you are in your right place, your dog will feel this too and dog training suddenly becomes so much easier and much more efficient.

Tree roots will never become boring or "mainstream". All tree roots are unique and create many different obstacles. Tree roots of fallen trees are the best, simply because they are bigger. Some roots are still very much attached to the ground creating slopes that you can train on. Others are very thick and are great for balance games. You can

also be lucky enough to find circular shapes to use for through games, or you might even play flying over some of the roots sticking up. Remember, when you are playing balance games on anything that is elevated from the ground to be ready to catch your dog in its harness, so it will not feel scared by suddenly losing its balance.

Fallen tree trunks are also amazing for many different dog parkour purposes. If the tree trunk is flat on the ground, beginners can use it for *balance games* and *flying games*. Depending on the height of the trunk, you can also play *bum in the air game* or *I'm the king game*. Advanced dogs can maybe even do the expert level of *bum in the air*

game where they back up onto the tree trunk with their hind body. If the tree trunk has fallen onto a hill creating a triangular shape, there will be a gap between the ground and the tree trunk. Depending on the size of the gap you can either practise *under the bridge games* or *through games*.

You can also use the trees as poles. You can create huge *slalom games* with the trees or have your dog run in a figure of 8 between two trees. *Time games* are also super useful in forests. You have so many different trees to use of different sizes. If your dog is an expert in the *time game*, try and combine the *time game* with *slalom games*. Have your dog run in circles around one tree, and when it finishes a whole circle, ask it to run to another tree and circle that instead. This looks super cool and you can vary the difficulty with different distances between the trees or different number of circles around the trees.

You can also use the healthy living trees for many awesome jumps or stands. You can teach your dog to jump up onto the tree and kick away from it again to land firmly on the ground. You can also teach your dog to stand tall against the tree with a *I'm the king game*, or for the advanced dogs you can try and ask them to do a *bum in the air game* against the tree.

The Countryside

The countryside

If you live at the countryside just like I've done my whole life, you can also find loads of exciting things in your environment which your dog can interact with and use to practise dog parkour. Depending on how your nearby countryside environment looks like, you might have to get a little creative though, but this is good practise for you as well. One of the most obvious obstacles you can use at the countryside for your dog parkour training are haybales.

Haybales come in many different forms and sizes, and you might have a sweet neighbour who will let you practise with the haybales on the

fields before they are picked up. Just remember to be polite and ask before using them. Haybales are great for *on top of the world games*, but if the haybales are very big compared to your dog then it is okay for you to lift it up on top of it. However, before you just start lifting your dog on top of tall objects, be sure to have practised this at home first so your dog is comfortable with you lifting it. As always, be ready to catch your dog in its harness if it should decide to try and jump down or simply step wrong on top of the haybale. It is not appropriate for all dogs to jump down from tall objects such as haybales. Keep the height of the object you are using and the size and health of your dog in mind before letting it jump down from obstacles.

While your dog is on top, you can ask it to perform different tricks like "twists," "waves," or "sit pretty" or general obedience commands such as alternating between "sit", "lie down", and "stand". You can also use them for *I'm the king games* and *bum in the air games*. Haybales are also great for *time games* and if they have been lined up you can play *slalom games* between them.

Some haybales also come in smaller sizes. These can be great for *elephant-like games* for the advanced dogs and *flying games* for the dogs who like to jump.

However, not everyone has access to haybales throughout the entire year, but some people on the countryside often have access to old machines or trailers. Depending on the machine you might be able to play *I'm the king games* or *bum in the air games*. With some machines you might also be able to play *under the bridge games, flying games* or *on the top of the world games.* If your dog is on expert level with its *time games,* you can try and have it circle a big machine. To make this easier for your dog the first time, make sure you have trained with many different sizes and shapes and gradually increased the difficulty. At first, try and praise and treat your dog for just running a few steps towards or around the machine. It might be difficult to place a treat in the exact position if the machine is quite big, but then try to use a toy instead. You can then throw the toy over the machine when you feel that your dog has run far enough.

Whenever you try to increase the difficulty of an exercise, remember to treat and praise more often than what you would normally do. So when you go a step forward in difficulty, you go a step back in endurance and timing of praise.

Trailers can also be quite fun. You can do all the above stuff with trailers too, but if the trailer has a triangular Y-shaped "attachment piece", you can have your dog do various things with this part of the trailer as well. You can either have your dog jump onto the attachment piece and gently walk across it and balance on it. You can have your dog do the *under the bridge game* with it. Alternatively, you can combine the two, by either starting to ask the dog to jump up onto the first beam of the Y, then walk down through the hole in the triangular Y-shape and then under the last beam, or the opposite way around.

Later on in the book, I will also cover how you can use old tires and how you can easily create your own dog parkour obstacles with them. But for now, I will just shortly give a few examples of what you can use old tires for if you have some lying around.

- If you place all of them side by side in a square, you can use them as on a military training track by stepping inside each tire. You can also run on top of the tires instead of stepping inside them.
- Use a single tire for *I'm the king games, bum in the air games,* or *on top of the world games.*
- If you have someone or something hold the tire vertically so it doesn't fall, you can use them for *through games.*

If you want more ideas now, then jump straight on to the "How to use tires" chapter.

Puppy Parkour

Puppy Parkour

As with any other physical dog sport, you have to be aware of your dog's age and physical well-being. As a puppy grows, its muscles, bones and joints are very fragile and you can easily end up with a dog who suffers from hip dysplasia if you train too much too early. However, it is also important for your puppy's development that they get to use their body so they can become more aware of their own body and movement. Dog parkour is not about how high your dog can jump anyway, so simply getting all the basics in place will allow for super efficient training and a fast learning dog when it gets older. Knowing all the basics will make it easier to further development the behaviours, so you should not feel tempted to try non-puppy-parkour things too early. Just enjoy the time with your puppy as long as it lasts and stick to the basic training. Also remember, that a puppy needs to sleep or rest around 20 hours a day and their ability to focus is limited. Refrain from training long sessions. Your puppy would prefer shorter sessions and then instead have them more often. You could potentially ditch the bowl (or at least use some of its food from the main meals) for your training. Therefore, you can start out slowly with gentle training and low and easy obstacles.

Platforms are great for puppy parkour but should not be higher than the dog's ankles (which is very low in a puppy's case) and you should not practise any jumps. Before practising proper dog parkour including jumps make sure your dog is at least one year old and preferably one and a half year old if your dog is of a bigger breed.

I'm the king games, bum in the air games, and *on top of the world games* are all suitable for puppy parkour. You just need to remember to use a proper sized platform so you do not strain your puppy's body unnecessarily. Also remember not to overdo these games or require too much from your puppy. Your puppy will love sticking to the basics and keeping it simple. As long as the games are simple and easy for the puppy to understand, they will absolutely love them!

Balance games on either platforms or fitness balls are also fine for puppy parkour. Just try to find one of those fitness balls that are halved and secured in a ring so it is not too tall and unstable. This will allow a height where the puppy will not be injured if it should decide to jump down from the ball without you expecting it. *Balance games* will help develop fine motor skills in your puppy, but as with everything else, it is important that you do not train it too much either. Since we are training with puppies, remember to also help your puppy as much as needed. We don't want them to become frustrated or insecure for any reason. So if the balance obstacle is moving a little bit, and your dog is feeling uncomfortable about it, try to keep the obstacle as steady as possible to help your dog have a success experience! Remember to give lots of treats to reinforce the behaviour.

Slalom games can also be used in puppy parkour as long as the slalom objects are not too close and the puppy is not *running* in slalom between them. If the dog is too excited and the slalom objects are too close to each other it could potentially injure itself with the rapid movements of jumping from side to side. Make sure your puppy is calm and has plenty of space between the slalom objects before starting your training. You can also use your hand as a target for your dog to follow. This can help slow down the dog if you think it is moving too fast.

Under the bridge games are also fine for puppy parkour as long as it has the space to stand up if it wants to. You should not force your puppy into a situation where it will have to crawl for a certain distance as the crawling behaviour can strain its body and joints.

Environment training

The most important part of puppy parkour is to environment train your puppy. This means that you will expose your puppy to many different objects, sounds and movements. Many things that seem so simple to us can be quite scary for a little puppy. I will therefore now come with a few suggestions as to what you can do to train environment training with your dog and ensure that it is exposed to many different things before reaching the age where everything new becomes dangerous.

Creating a sensing field is great for puppy environment training. A sensing field is basically just a small area where you have spread out many, many different objects on the ground. It could be everything from kitchen tools and appliances, to children's toys, to garden tools (both big and small ones), to clothing items, to old bottles of glass and plastic. Then also spread out some delicious treats on top of or underneath the many different items in the sensing field. Now let your puppy sniff out all the treats and let it step on everything it wants to step on. There might be items that move upon touch or some that makes a certain sound. All this helps the dog build up a glossary of items it has seen before and knows are not dangerous. This will increase its confidence and lower any fears and anxieties it might otherwise develop. If you know, that your dog is already afraid of a certain object, then put it somewhere in all the mess with lots of treats around it. Maybe the dog will even go get the treats and start ignoring the otherwise dangerous item.

Bring your dog to a quiet little city with only just a few cars, some bicycles and maybe a few trains to get your dog used to many different environments and noises. Make sure to bring lots of treats with you for this and praise your dog very often. If you are not used to living in the city with your dog, then do not expect your dog to be as obedient as it usually is. This is totally fine and you should not get mad about it. The dog is simply taking in all the different smells and noises that it is not used to, and it might just be too much to also be able to focus on you. This is all about giving the dog a good experience among the sounds of a city, not about behaving like a 10 year old dog that has lived in the city its entire life. Let your puppy be a puppy and simply let it have a positive experience in the city. If the small city visit goes well you can try gradually building up to larger and larger cities with more and more noise.

Putting a tarpaulin on the ground can seem simple and downright weird to us. However, puppies are not yet used to walking on many different surfaces. A surface that then also makes a specific sound when you walk on it can therefore seem very scary to a puppy. Throw some treats onto the tarpaulin and let your puppy go get them. It might be startled the first time it steps on the tarpaulin but that is totally fine. Let it just take its time. If it does not seek back onto the tarpaulin, try to walk on it yourself, sit down on it and start counting treats. Verbally praise your puppy when it approaches the tarpaulin again and starts walking onto it. Letting your puppy walk on something that creates a specific noise is called "active noise". This is a concept that you have to teach your dog as it is not an understanding that it is born with.

Active noise

Active noise is when a sound is the consequence of something you do. So if you touch a piano, it makes a sound. Understanding that it is yourself who caused the sound and not caused by something or someone else, is the definition of the concept. Teaching your dog to understand this concept early can help prevent unpleasant surprises and fears. This also applies to noisy toys or when your dog tips something and it falls down.

My next advice might go against what you have originally thought you should be doing. I want you to encourage your puppy to make noise. Of course, no one wants a dog that barks all the time, so we are not teaching our dog to bark. What I want you to do is to experiment with active noise. Introduce your dog to situations where there are lots of reinforcers, but in order to get to them the puppy will have to walk or search through something that makes a noise. For starters, this could be hiding treats in a playpen among a lot of small plastic balls. You can also use a lot of empty soda cans and fill them with small stones and rocks and tape over the opening so the dog doesn't cut itself on it. Then put all the cans in a bucket or in a pile on the ground and drizzle some treats under and over the cans for the dog to find. When the dog goes searching for the treats it will push the cans which will then make a sound. Try to come up with 3 different active noise activities yourself.

Advanced Dog Parkour

Advanced dog parkour

Now we have covered all the fun basic core games and our dogs LOVE it! When our dogs start showing us that they have great confidence in both themselves and in you, then we are ready to kick it up a notch and further develop our games. All of the basic core games have their own expert level games as well. So if your dog excels in one or two of the core games but aren't on expert level with the other games, then you can still play the more advanced game versions of the ones your dog is good at. Your dog doesn't have to be an expert in all the games before moving on to some of the expert level games. So have a go at some expert level FUN!

I'm the King expert level game challenges:

The first thing you want to do to challenge your dog more in this game is to change how it associates you with the game. For now it might have a picture in its head of this game being associated with you standing a certain way right next to the object. That means, if you try to change this picture by for example standing in a different way, your dog might not recognise the game. Therefore, we want to spice it up.

Challenge #1 – walk around

The first expert level game challenge is about getting you to move all the way around your dog in a circle while it stays in position. If you have been playing the basic game enough, this is actually a quite simple change to make to the game. Start by simply shifting your weight from one leg to the other and praise your dog for keeping the position. Remember to give it a release cue once in a while to keep up the excitement in the game. Gradually lean more and more onto one of your legs and take a small step. Keep placing the treat the exact same place every time, so your dog doesn't spin around to look after you when you start walking. You want it to keep looking in the same direction as it started. The better you are at upholding these criteria for the dog, the easier it actually finds the game. If you are inconsistent in your criteria, like sometimes do not mind the dog turning its head around after you, and then other times only praising for looking straight ahead, the rules of the game become too confusing for the dog and it might step down from its platform in confusion. When you can get behind your dog you give an extra good praise and maybe even a release cue to kick up the excitement. This is the hardest part of the new challenge to the game because your dog really wants to look at and turn towards you. So praise it for choosing not to.

Main points:

- Start by shifting weight from side to side
- Gradual approach to more and more steps
- Place your reinforcer the exact same place as before in relation to the dog – not to you
- Release once in a while to keep excitement up!
- Keep your criteria clear and simple

Challenge #2 – be a clown

Now we are able to walk around our dog while it maintains its position. Now we want to change our own behaviour even more. Ideally, we want to be able to do anything, no matter how stupid we look, and the dog should still stay in its position. So start by doing something relatively easy – lift up your arm. Praise the dog if it stays. Then lift the other arm. Then both arms. If this is successful, try moving your arms around. Gradually put more and more movement into your own body, but be aware that you do not move ahead too quickly. You do not want to set your dog up for failure. If your dog is just super good at this, try to sit or lie down on the ground – maybe even roll around. True experts can jump around and make a fool of themselves while their dog patiently stays in its position – most likely wondering what has gotten into you.

Main points:

- Gradual approach to moving your body more and more
- Do not move ahead too quickly
- PRAISE your GOOD dog!

Challenge #3 – Elephant

Since we are now able to move around as much as we want, we now want our dog to move around the object while still maintaining the game. I call this "Elephant" because it looks like what elephants were asked to do in circuses – two paws on top of the object while the two hind paws are still on the ground and circling the object. For this game I prefer to use a low bucket or a small or round dishwashing bowl. The round shape makes it easier for the dog to circle the object while standing on it. You can always transfer this game's skills to other objects when your dog first has mastered the behaviour. I will also recommend practising this exercise a lot to improve the hind body control of the dog. This will help in many other exercises where the hind body is the dominant part – such as backing exercises, backwards slaloms, backwards circles or side steps.

As with many of our other games, you can play them in two different ways in the beginning – by luring or shaping. If you prefer shaping, and if your dog either has a "what can you do"-command or in another way knows the difference between you waiting for a new behaviour to happen and simply practising endurance training, this will be a fun and easy task. Get your dog to stand in the I'm the King position, and give your dog a treat. While giving the treat, you have to move yourself behind your dog, so your dog is standing with its back towards you. The treat is simply a distraction so you can get in a position where it is easiest for your dog to offer the wanted behaviour. We help our dog this way to avoid any frustration or major confusion. When your dog has eaten the treat, it will realise that you are no longer standing in front of it. If the dog knows that it is allowed to move, it will most likely try to turn around to get eye contact with you again. Here you have to be quick and click (or praise in any other fast and accurate way) for simply taking ONE small step while its front paws are still on the bucket. If your dog steps down, you might have been too slow to click for the behaviour and your dog has gotten confused. Most dogs won't directly jump down from the bucket but take at least one or two steps with their hind paws before getting down, so if you are quick enough at clicking for this behaviour, your dog won't go down from the bucket. Repeat the above steps with varying amounts of paw-steps before clicking. Soon you will have a dog that walks smoothly in a half circle. If the half circle is in place, and if you have been clicking for varying amounts of steps, you can simply wait with your clicker until your dog offers just a single step more than the half circle towards the full circle. If your dog just seems to never do more than the half circle, no matter how long you have been practising this with varying amounts of steps, you can try and combine your training methods with the luring technique below.

Main points:

- Start with your dog in the normal I'm the King position
- Use your treat as a distraction to get behind your dog
- Let your dog know it is free to move
- Await just a single step with the hind paws and CLICK!
- Repeat many times with varying amounts of steps
- Remember a release cue once in a while

If you find it easier to lure your dog, then here is what you should do. If your dog knows how to use your hand as a target to follow, then use that, otherwise lure with a treat in your hand or pretend to have one if your dog gets too distracted by the real thing. Start with the dog in the normal I'm the King position and praise it. Now, with your luring hand somewhere around the dog's face, try to lure your dog to move. Some dogs prefer if you hold your hand above their head and simply turn your wrist. Others find it easier if you place your hand on one of the sides of the dog's face. Praise as soon as you see a slight shift in balance or a proper step with one of the hind paws. Some dogs might be able to take several steps already, and that is fine to do that, but remember to praise early so your dog doesn't accidentally step down from the bucket in confusion. Do this loads of times and praise for varying numbers of steps. When your dog gets to the point where it is going to pass in front of you, make sure to step a little bit backwards to allow sufficient space for your dog. If your dog bounces into your leg, you might surprise it and end up having trouble getting it to walk pass you in the game again. When your dog is moving more smoothly in this exercise, you can try to fade away your luring hand by moving it higher and higher above the dog's head and simply transfer the movement of your hand into a twist in your wrist or by doing circles in the air with one of your fingers. Put in a verbal cue when the fluency is getting better, and soon you won't need your hand signal anymore. When your dog knows the elephant challenge in one direction on verbal cue, try to teach it to walk in the other direction as well with a different verbal cue.

Main points:

- Start in the normal I'm the King position
- Lure your dog by placing your hand in different ways in relation to its face
- Praise for slight shifts of balance or single movements of hind paws
- Vary the amounts of steps required before praising
- Give your dog enough space to pass in front of you
- Fade out your hand signal by making it smaller or moving it somewhere else

Challenge #4 – team up

When your dog has mastered the elephant challenge, I can guarantee you that your dog now has a much better awareness of its hind body and better motor skills. Now we want to use these skills and its new-found confidence in the more advanced game to make it all seem even more impressive and to challenge our best friend a little bit more. What we want to do now is to combine challenge 1 and 3. While your dog plays the elephant challenge, you will walk around your dog and its obstacle in the opposite direction of what the dog is moving.

Remember, when you start this exercise, your dog will most likely get confused if you just start walking the opposite way around it while it tries to do the elephant challenge. Therefore, as mentioned earlier in the book, whenever you want to increase the difficulty and take an extra step forward, you have to take a few steps back with regard to endurance training and how long you wait before giving a treat. So while your dog does the elephant challenge, you take a few steps around your dog (maybe even only a single step depending on the dog's own confidence in the game) and then you praise your dog for still moving. If your dog stops moving, simply wait until it offers at least one more step again – and THEN praise. Do this a couple of times with varying amounts of steps around your dog – just remember to only praise the dog while it is still moving. If you have played the second challenge enough, your dog shouldn't find this too difficult either, as it is used to you acting weird while maintaining its own game.

Main points:

- Remember to praise more often the first many times you play this game
- Let your dog start doing the elephant challenge
- Take a few steps around your dog
- Always praise the dog while it is moving and NOT if it is standing still

- If it is too difficult, try combining the second challenge with the third challenge before doing this one

Challenge #5 – All 'round

The last challenge for this game is actually quite simple. This challenge is more a challenge for you than for your dog. You will have to come up with as many different ways you can think of to use the *I'm the King game*. Think of all the different obstacles you can use for this game in your nearby environment. When you have done your own environment, try to think of some in a different environment BEFORE you go visit it. When you then do go visit that environment, see if there were any obstacles or different ways of using this game that you hadn't thought about. Make a list of all the different objects you can use for the game and how to generalise your dog's behaviour. Then slowly start ticking them off with your dog.

The Balance game expert level challenges:

Once your dog has gotten comfortable with the normal balance games, you can further improve its balance and boost its confidence by help it to overcome new challenges and build a better awareness of how it can relocate its weight for different purposes. Training balance exercises can also greatly improve a healthy amount of muscle mass.

Challenge #1 - Wiggle wiggle

Now that your dog is definitely comfortable being on top of other objects no matter if you trained "on top of the world" or "balance games" with it, you'll now be able to challenge it a bit further and truly experience the dog developing a sense of 'balance'.

This first challenge is not about having your dog walk on tall obstacles. This is about actually *developing* a balance ability in your dog. Having a sense of balance is not always something you just have - often it needs to be developed through experience. The best way to do this would be to use a balance (BOSU) ball. Start super simple by asking your dog to get all four paws on top of the balance ball. Already now, your dog might be experiencing difficulties keeping its balance. This will look like the dog is shaking. Keep feeding your dog delicious treats for standing there and praise lots verbally. The reason it is shaking is not necessarily because it is scared. Often, this is simply the dog's muscles contracting at different times in relation to each other because the dog is trying to find its balance. Once it stops "shaking" it has found the correct balance point, which means it has adjusted the distribution of its weight correctly throughout its body. This is what we want to work towards.

For some dogs, the next step will be more difficult, whereas for others it can actually help them figure out how to distribute its weight properly. For this next step, try and ask your dog to either shake a paw with you or wave at you. This way the dog will have to redistribute its weight onto only three legs. For some dogs this is difficult, and for others this help them realise what they need to do in order to stand more comfortably on the balance ball. Remember now, that if you ask your dog to wave while balancing, it is important to praise for even the smallest lift of its paw as it might be surprised how difficult it is to keep its balance while doing this - thereby reinforce the dog so it knows that this is correct even though it feels weird.

You can also use human balance/wiggle boards with either two front paws, two hind paws, or all 4 paws on top for a different type of balance training. These can both be used to make the exercise easier and more difficult - so have a go!

Main points:

- Get your dog to stand with all 4 paws on top of a balance ball
- Praise it to make it more comfortable
- Either let it figure out itself that it has to distribute its weight differently to stand comfortably, or ask it for a paw shake or a wave to show it how to redistribute its weight.
- Remember to praise for even the smallest lifts of the paws when asking it to wave on top of a balance ball.

Challenge #2 - Superdog

Once your dog has become super good at the first challenge and has discovered its sense of balance, you can further improve this ability by making it a little more challenging. Remember, you know your own dog best, so be sure to respect the level your dog is at so you do not pressure it into doing something that is too difficult too early. There is also no one who is telling you that you HAVE to complete all challenges - make sure to always keep your training fun, and if there are some things you would rather not do, then no one is judging you! When this is said - the next challenge is actually not that more difficult if you just help your dog.

Most balance (BOSU) balls have a hard surface underneath which is used for improving the balance in people by having them either sit or stand on this hard surface with the ball facing downwards. Now the ball will make it much more difficult to balance on the hard surface if it is not supported by someone or something.

Start out by securing the upside-down balance ball in such a way, that it does not move too much when you step on it. You can either place it in a corner, or hold it with your hands. You can also use a helper and have them hold the balance ball while you focus on your dog.

Ask your dog to get on top of the hard surface. Make sure the dog is feeling comfortable before proceeding. Once your dog is ready, you can loosen the grip on the ball slightly (but not all at once!) so it starts feeling the need for redistributing its weight according to the movement of the ball. Praise lots as soon as there is the slightest movement in the ball. It is entirely up to you how far you want to take this exercise, but you could try to work towards the dog being able to stand on the hard surface without anyone supporting the ball - maybe even while doing certain tricks. It is also, however, a huge accomplishment just being able to have the dog standing rather comfortably on top of the hard surface while someone is just slightly supporting the ball! You can also do this with only two front paws or two hind paws if you want to focus building muscles or awareness in a specific part of the dog's body.

This can also be done using small paw pods if you want to just focus on balance in the anterior or posterior part of the body. When using the paw pods your dog's body wont be raised so much from the ground relative to the part of the body that is still on the ground if you are only working with two paws.

Main points:

- Turn the balance ball upside-down.
- Support the balance ball so it does not move.
- Ask the dog to get on top.
- Slowly loosen the grip on the balance ball to get the dog balancing.
- Praise lots as soon as the ball starts moving slightly.
- Take it as far as your dog feels comfortable.

The time game expert level challenges:

When your dog has mastered the basic Time game and can perform a full circle around a pole-like object with fluency you are ready for taking on some expert challenges!

Challenge #1 – Keep going

The first challenge is about getting our dog to perform several circles around the pole instead of just one. The method is actually quite simple, but depending on your dog and its experience with this kind of method, you might have to be patient.

All you need to do is to ask your dog to go round the pole. When it finishes, you don't say anything, you simply just wait for the dog to either go for an extra round or just offer a few steps in the right direction. Some dogs, if they are familiar with this method, they just keep going until you praise them. Others might stop up and wait for their treat, and if it doesn't come after some time, they might offer to do the behaviour once more as to say "Didn't you see me do it, human?". Other dogs might get really confused about the situation, so you might only get a very small extra step in the right direction, and then you praise for that by throwing the treat further around the clock. At some point, the dog will understand that it just has to keep going until you praise it.

Some dogs, however, do not only get confused, but they can become easily frustrated. For these dogs, it might not be the best method to just wait for them to offer the behaviour again, despite the final outcome being better. For these dogs, you might have to give them an extra cue in order to get them going. If you DO give an extra cue, then you should also praise the dog for any steps it might take after that, otherwise you can ultimately end up ruining the basic game you have been working on. But before trying this method, try the first one and be patient. Your dog might give a few barks, but that is okay. As long as it doesn't totally block out everything and start a constant barking session.

Main points:

- Ask your dog to walk around the pole like normally
- Wait and see if it offers to do more than the one full circle
- Praise in the right time-game manner around the clock
- If your dog gets frustrated, help it out

Challenge #2 – Generalising

When your dog knows the game with poles, then why not try and spice it up with other objects as well? They don't even have to be round! If you really feel up for a challenge, try using another person or even a dog as the obstacle! Just make sure that the dogs like each other, and that the other dog is staying in a sit or stand so it doesn't suddenly start walking while your dog is trying to walk around it.

Challenge #3 – Long time

Try to increase the distance between you and the object you want your dog to walk around. Remember to praise more often, whenever you increase the difficulty for the dog. So be ready to throw some treats! Keep varying the distance between you and the obstacle. Don't always just increase the distance, as the dog will not think this is fun.

Challenge #4 – 8 o'clock

Combine your dog's fine time games with a basic slalom-like game. Ask your dog to complete a full circle or two around one obstacle and then send it straight to another nearby obstacle to circle that as well. If you keep going it will look like your dog is running in a figure of 8. Try and do a full and easy circle with each of the obstacles before combining them both into this game challenge. This will help the dog better understand that it is in fact supposed to use both obstacles.

Now when your dog is confident in jumping up onto a platform it would be pretty cool if your dog could also do stuff while being on top of the platform, right? So let's look at a few challenges.

Challenge #1 – Trick 'n' Treat

While being on top of platforms it is pretty cool if you can perform tricks as well. If you don't know any tricks already, hop on to the chapter about useful tricks. Here I would just like to share some advice with regard to performing tricks on top of platforms.

If your trick requires the dog to move, make sure that the platform is not too tall with only little space. The dog will be super excited to do tricks, and if it should step wrong it might fall down if you haven't taken the available space into account.

When you first want to teach your dog to perform tricks on top of platforms, you should first have generalised the wanted trick behaviour as much as possible, so you can act like a clown around your dog while it still offers the trick. The same kind of generalisation should have been achieved with the platform behaviour before you start combining the two. This ensures a much better performance of the trick on top of the platform, and your dog will be much more aware of its own body as well which may help prevent being unsuccessful in the performance. It is also important to remember to give it time. Your dog might not be comfortable doing tricks on platforms just yet, but it will come with time. If you just keep practising and only ask for the trick behaviours that it is super confident in, your dog will soon be able to perform magnificent tricks on top of platforms or anywhere else in general.

Main points:

- Take all safety measures into account before asking your dog to perform tricks on platforms
- Make sure your trick behaviour is generalised enough
- Make sure your dog is confident enough in the platform behaviours
- It helps if the dog has great self-awareness
- Be patient and always use the dog's favourite and most confident tricks first

Challenge #2 – Parkour dog

I have mentioned earlier, that dog parkour is not about getting your dog to jump from rooftop to rooftop. However, if you find an environment where it will be possible and safe to jump from one obstacle to another obstacle this can be quite fun and it looks super impressive!

First you have to make sure that it really IS safe for your dog to do this challenge. Is your dog physically able to perform these jumps? If it is an older dog or a very young dog, you should refrain from doing this. You should also notice how tall the obstacles are. I will never recommend doing this challenge on any obstacles that are taller than the dog itself. Your dog might very well be able to do this just fine, no matter the height, but you have to keep in mind, IF something should happen the damage will be greater the taller the obstacles are. Another very important thing to check before asking your dog to perform this challenge is to have a look at the surface of the obstacle. Is it slippery or will it be difficult to get a proper foothold? How narrow are the obstacles where the dog is supposed to land? Would it be sensible and responsible to ask the dog to jump here? Also, is the distance between the two alright, or is it too far? Remember, if the dog is tired or if the weather is bad, do not expect your dog to be able to jump as far as it normally can. You should also look out for any potential distractions for the dog.

If you want to do this challenge, you should start with obstacles that are very close together (almost normal stepping distance) and obstacles that have a nice and big surface to land on. When your dog is getting really good at stepping or hopping from one obstacle to the other you can slowly increase the difficulty of ONE of the two factors above. Do not both increase the distance between the obstacles as well as the size and foothold properties of the surface at the same time. If you find it difficult to find obstacles where you can manipulate the difficulty in your nearby environment, you can practise on big bricklayer's bowls which are sold in most handyman shops.

If your dog is jumping down on the ground before jumping up onto the next obstacle it is their way to say that they are either not feeling comfortable about the landing obstacle or that the distance is too big. If this happens, take a step back in difficulty and place the obstacles very close together so your dog can practically just walk across. When it has become confident in doing this, you can try to increase the distance with a maximum of 5 cm. When your dog is confident about this distance you can increase by 5 cm again. Do not go too far too fast. It is better to prevent the dog from getting the idea that it can just step down as it can be more difficult if it has already figured out that it can get to the other obstacle by doing that.

Main points:

- Make sure that it is safe for your dog to perform this challenge
- Start with the obstacles very close together
- Do not increase distance and surface properties at the same time
- Prevent the dog from getting the idea to jump down in between the obstacles by going slow
- Increase distance with only 5cm at a time

Challenge #3 - Stepping stones

Just like the above challenge, this one is about moving from one obstacle to another. This is different in the way, that there are more obstacles which are also closer together, and the surface is only big enough to fit a single paw – or two if the dog has really great balance. This can be done with small tree stumps put close together for children to walk on, or by having a lot of vertical standing or horizontal lying tires put down next to each other. You can also use big stones or rocks, but you have to be certain that they won't move and that they are easy and comfortable to step on.

The way to teach this is pretty much the same as the one above. You just have to remember to maybe move a bit slower as the dog needs to take its time to place its paws right. If the obstacles are too far apart the dog might also choose to get down, so make sure that it is easier for the dog to choose to stay on top of the obstacles than it is to walk down in between. With time and experience you can place the obstacles further apart, but remember never to place them so far apart that the dog can't reach them by simply stretching their legs a bit. This challenge should not encourage any jumps of any kind as that can be dangerous on such small and narrow stepping stones.

Challenge #4 – Ladders

You can also use ladders in many different ways. Ladders can be great fun and it doesn't even have to be difficult. You can easily adjust the difficulty when playing with ladders, so let me introduce you to some of the many ways you can use ladders. You might even be able to come up with more and new ways yourself.

Walking in between the steps.

When working with ladders it's often easiest if you place it on top of a few blocks so it is raised just about 5 cm off the ground. This helps the dog differentiate between the ground and the ladder. For this first exercise we want the dog to step over each step on the ladder and walk on the ground in between the steps. You can have your dog walk over all of the steps, or if you raise the ladder a bit, have it walk or jump over every second one and then crawl under the other ones.

Depending on the distance between each step on the ladder and the size of your dog, you can also ask your dog to perform different tricks every time it has stepped over the ladder and is in one of the "holes".

Walking on the ladder

The next thing you can do is to teach your dog to walk on top of the ladder. Again, it is easiest if you place the ladder on top of something that raises it approximately 5 cm off the ground. Then first let your dog feel the steps of the ladder by asking it to put its front paws on the first step. Praise it and ask it to move a bit forward. It is easiest to lure this behaviour, so either use your hand as a follow target or have a treat ready for your dog.

When it has all four paws up praise it again a couple of times before trying to move on. Remember, the more you reinforce a behaviour, the more confident the dog becomes in that behaviour. If you move too fast, the dog might not feel comfortable and it might become insecure about the exercise and then jump down prematurely. Therefore, support your dog through all the small steps of every exercise and reinforce plenty on the way! When your dog is confident in standing on the ladder, you can try to move a little bit forward yourself. If the dog doesn't follow, try to lure with your hand.

Main points:

- Place ladder on top of 5cm blocks and make sure it is stabilised
- First have your dog to walk over every step to get your dog to be comfortable around the ladder
- Then try to ask your dog to walk on the steps
- Start with just two paws
- Praise for all the small steps
- Vary your training by getting your dog to alternate between walking over and under the steps
- Always be ready to catch your dog in its harness if it walks on top of the ladder. If it crawls under it, it might be easier without a leash as to not getting the dog entangled in the ladder.

Bum in the air game expert level challenges

For this game I am only going to demonstrate two expert level challenges, but they can both be transferred onto almost anything else, where only your own imagination sets limits. With these challenges you simply need to remember to train them slowly and not too often in the beginning as they require a lot of muscles in the dog's front and upper body, especially around the shoulders, chest and what would be the dog's biceps. As your dog gets more confident in these exercises, the more muscle mass will the dog also have. With more muscle mass and a better understanding of how to use the different muscles, the exercises will become easier for the dog. But even though, they might seem easy for your dog, do not train it too often or for too long sessions. You should also be aware that dogs can become sore just like humans after working out. So occasionally giving your dog a good and thorough massage can help prevent any soreness.

Figure 3 - Dog backing up against a tree.

Challenge #1 – up, up, up

For this first challenge we are going to use a platform designed to fit the size of your dog. This means that it is only as long as the distance between the front and hind paws of your dog, and only as wide as the dog's shoulders. The purpose of this challenge is ultimately to teach our dogs to walk backwards up onto something vertical.

Start by placing your platform perpendicular to your dog, so the dog has a wide area to use. Then you lure your dog over the platform until it stands with its hind legs on the platform and its front legs on the ground. Then you praise several times for this position and give your dog a release cue, preferably behind the platform to start with. Hopefully your dog will resume the previous position, otherwise you help it again by luring it into the right position. Praise again. Repeat these steps until the dog automatically resumes the right position at least 8 out of 10 times. Even if the release treat was thrown somewhere else than right behind the platform.

Figure 4 - Dog standing with two hind paws on the platform, and two front paws on the ground.

Now move your dog right in front of the perpendicular platform and simply wait and see if the dog offers to just take a small single step backwards. Praise your dog for standing in the same position as before or for offering a single step backwards towards the platform depending on how far in the training your dog is. Praise the dog and release the dog again and now throw the treat right in front of the dog, so it will still face you and stand between you and the platform instead of getting behind the platform. Let it resume the right position by moving backwards.

If your dog does not resume the wanted position it can sometimes in this case help to change your own body position, so instead of standing up right in front of the dog which can be perceived unpleasantly for some dogs, try to sit down on the floor and spread out your legs, so you end up forming a triangle with your legs and the platform. Then keep the dog inside this triangle and have it face you. Since you are not standing up and is no longer perceived as a little intimidating, the dog might find it easier to work with you and thereby offer the backwards behaviour. When the right backing behaviour leads to the right position 8 out of 10 times, you can start adding a verbal cue for this behaviour.

When the above behaviour is strong and consistent you start elevating the platform by placing books (or equivalent) under it. This is to teach the dog to lift its hind legs a bit more and start crawling backwards up vertical structures. Do this until the dog is able to walk onto the platform with its hind paws while there are two books under it.

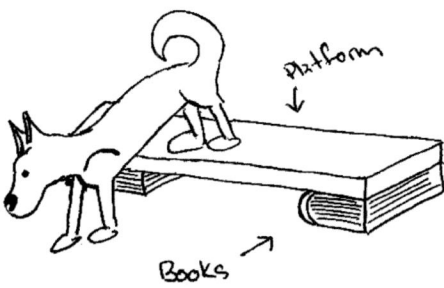

Figure 5 - Place books underneath the platform to elevate it slightly.

Once your dog is confident and consistent in the steps above, you should start to turn the platform around so it is in a straight line with your dog. Ask your dog to perform the backwards moving behaviour and praise your dog for getting into the right position with the two hind paws on the platform. Depending on your dog's accuracy it might not hit the platform at first, but keep trying a couple of times. If the dog really does not hit the platform, turn the platform around again or find a platform that is a little bit wider. The reason why we want to keep the platform narrow is to improve the accuracy of the dog's movement to prevent it from turning its body sideways to the obstacle instead of walking up the vertical structure in a straight line. If your dog is able to do the behaviour in a straight line, then start putting books underneath the end of the platform that is furthest away from the dog so the platform stands with a certain gradient. Gradually and slowly increase this gradient until you are ultimately able to put the platform against a wall and finally have the platform standing vertically against the wall as well. As the very final step, you start to phase out the platform and have the dog walk up the wall backwards.

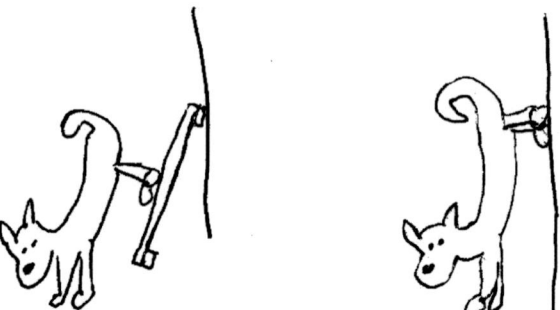

Figure 6 - Gradually increase the steepness of the platform until you are able to ask your dog to walk backwards up a vertical structure.

If you want to, this is also the way you teach your dog to do a handstand, but since the handstand is without any support and puts a lot of strain on the dog's body I will not recommend teaching your dog to do it in case you accidentally put too much pressure on the dog. Always have some kind of support for the dog to use.

Main points:

- Place your platform perpendicular to your dog and lure it into the right position
- Using release cues, let the dog resume the right position numerous times before advancing
- Encourage backing behaviour by placing the dog in front of the platform
- Elevate the platform with books
- Try to turn the platform to increase accuracy in the backing behaviour
- Gradually and slowly increase the elevation of one of the sides of the platform

- Finally place the platform against a wall, making it more and more vertical

Challenge #2 – bow wow

The bow wow challenge is basically an opposite elephant exercise. It requires great hind body control and some front body muscle. The final exercise consists of the dog having its two hind legs on the dishwashing bowl while having its two front legs on the ground. It will then with its front legs move around the bucket in a circle while maintaining the bow position. If your dog is small, very young, old, or has a bad back or shoulders, you can still do this exercise in a simpler way by turning the bowl around, so the dog simply stands inside it instead of bowing on top of it.

This is easiest if your dog is already familiar working with the bowl from the expert level challenges of the *I'm the King game*. For this challenge, we actually start with our dog exactly as in *I'm the king game*. Now we just want to teach it a face-to-face exercise. This means, that your dog will always stay in a straight line with you, looking directly up at you. If you then move around the bucket, your dog will follow in such a way, that it will stand in front of you again and keep looking up at you.

Teaching the face-to-face exercise is actually pretty simple, but it might take some time before the dog is ready to transfer the behaviour into other situations. Have the dog on the bucket as described above and give a treat for standing in a straight line with you, looking up at you. Praise like this several times so the dog gets the idea that standing like this triggers the treat-giving. Furthermore, the dog is developing muscle memory for the mental image it is creating of the situation. Now you can try to move a single or a few steps to one side, and hopefully your dog will also move a few steps with its hind body in order to face you again. If it doesn't move, then wait until it does. It might not be completely straight the first couple of times, but praise when it moves, and then help it into the exact position it is supposed to be in. Helping the dog into the right position and then giving treats helps with the developing muscle memory of the exercise. You just have to maintain the criteria yourself, otherwise the dog will not be able to develop accurate muscle memory and it won't understand the exercise. So be clear and consistent in your criteria and help the dog if it doesn't understand the exercise.

When your dog is good at keeping the criteria of the face-to-face exercise, you should be able to do the same, while the dog is standing with the hind legs on top op the bucket instead. Start with just a single step that the dog has to follow, and praise greatly for this. Remember, even though your dog might be excellent at the normal face-to-face exercise, you have just changed the picture of the exercise for the dog. The dog's muscle memory does not recognise the position it is standing in and it can be difficult to understand the association between your face-to-face command and the bow-like position. Take your time and praise for every single step. Soon you'll be able to either shape or lure the rest of the circle without you having to move around with it.

Main points:

- Make sure your dog is already familiar with the normal elephant exercise
- Teach your dog the face-to-face exercise
- Get your dog to stand in the wanted position on the bucket with two hind paws on top and two front paws on the ground while facing you
- Ask it to keep being face-to-face with you and then move a few steps (or a single) and see if the dog maintains the criteria
- Praise for maintaining criteria
- Gradually move more and more around the bucket
- When this is easy for the dog, put on a verbal cue
- Now either shape or lure the behaviour with the cue as help without you moving along with it

Under the bridge game expert level challenge

For this game I only have a single expert level challenge for you. You can however easily make it even more difficult by simply including basic obedience commands between your *under the bridge games*.

Challenge #1 – sneaking

The purpose of this challenge is to get our dog to crawl in open space with no objects to crawl under.

You start by having your dog lying in front of you. With a treat in your hand you now simply lure your dog to crawl. When trying to lure this behaviour it is important to keep your hand close to the ground and moving slowly. Otherwise, you risk the dog standing up instead of crawling. If you feel like your dog is on the way to get up, simply stop moving your hand and wait for the dog to lie down again. Always praise while the dog is lying down or while moving without the bum being up too high.

When your dog is starting to get the hang of it you can introduce a verbal cue while you lure your dog. Later on, use the verbal cue and then start luring with your hand, but now without any treats in it. Soon you will be able to use your hand less and less, or at least move it quicker, and this is the beginning of phasing out your own body language in the exercise.

Depending on how you would like your finished trick to look like (i.e., crawling in a straight line, or crawling in a circle around you), you can use different targets for the dog to move towards.

If you want your dog to crawl in a straight line without you moving along with it as a support, you can use a blanket. Whenever you train the crawling behaviour, make sure that the behaviour then ends on the blanket where the dog is rewarded with lots of treats for lying down. You are allowed to praise it during the crawling behaviour as well to reinforce the movement rather than only the end position.

Slowly you can start to move the blanket further and further away and have the dog crawl longer in order to get there. When you start to be able to phase out your hand, you might be able to have the dog crawl alone for a few centimetres onto the blanket. Then you slowly start working with increasing the distance now without any hand signals. Just remember, when you want to phase out your hand signal you cannot also work on increasing the distance to the blanket. That will be too difficult for the dog. So when you want to phase out your hand signal, the blanket should be very close to the dog.

You can also use a platform (accustomed to the dog's size) if your dog prefers this way of training. Teach your dog to go onto the platform and lie down on it facing away from you in a straight line (you standing behind the platform). In the beginning you just teach it to lie down on the platform. Then you start to move around the platform eventually standing behind it while asking the dog to walk onto the platform and lie down while facing away from you. Always give the treats in front of the dog's nose so it will not have to look at you as this can potentially ruin the exercise. Give this special "down" a special cue as well. When the dog is good at this special down on the platform, you transfer it onto the ground by using a blanket cut to the same size as the platform. When the dog can perform the special down on the blanket consistently, you can try without the blanket. When the dog is then finally consistent in the special down on bare ground, you are read to try and incorporate it into the crawling exercise. Have the dog crawl a few centimetres and then give it a special down. You then keep alternating between these two cues. The special down is to ensure that the dog will continue to crawl straight ahead without you moving with it. Otherwise, you might end up with a dog that will gradually turn more and more towards you while crawling.

If you want your dog to crawl around you in a single you can start by sitting down on the ground with your dog. While luring your dog to crawl, you just lure your dog around you. Slowly, you can begin to stand up more and more while still luring your dog a bit in order to help it. Soon you will be able to stand up fully while having your dog crawl around you. Just be aware that some dogs tend to "cheat" while they are behind their owner, so make sure that you reinforce the dog enough to stay down when it is behind you. Keeping the criteria clear all the time helps prevent the dog from making mistakes.

Main points:

- Have your dog lying in front of you
- With a treat in your hand, lure your dog to crawl
- Praise while the dog is either lying down or in movement but staying close to the ground
- Stop your dog from standing up by stopping moving your hand
- When crawling is easier, introduce verbal cue
- Teach your dog to crawl straight ahead or in a circle around you

The through game and *the flying game* expert level challenges

For these last advanced dog parkour challenges I have chosen to combine the two games "through" and "flying" for some of the exercises. Here I want to teach you how to teach your dog to jump over your back and through a circle you make with your arms. The fun thing is, it is actually pretty simple and straight forward.

Challenge #1 – fly over the hill

First I want to teach you how to get your dog to jump over your back. Please, again remember that any jumping games and challenges are not for dogs under at least 12 months old, and you should evaluate your own dog's physique before doing any big jumps. If you are in doubt, it is better to refrain from playing these exact games or potentially seek a veterinary opinion.

For these challenges you need a standard agility jump. Set up the jump equipment and get your dog to jump over a few times until it really understands what you are doing. Try to get your dog to jump without you running with it, so either stand back and ask the dog to jump ahead or stand right next to the jump and call your dog to jump. The important thing here is that the dog does not return to you to get the treat right after the jump as we want the dog to land securely on its feet as far away from the jump as possible. The dog should also be able to perform the jump on verbal cue only. Use a distance rewarder or have a helper ready to cover the treat you have placed away from the jump.

When your dog does not need you to run with it in order to perform a good-looking jump, you can now involve yourself in the exercise. Lie down on your knees with your head bend down under the jump-pole. Crouch down as much as possible to make the jump as low as possible to begin with. Have your dog sit a few feet in front of you awaiting your next command. Ask your dog to jump, just as you did before, and have it fly over you. If it doesn't seem to understand the exercise, have your helper help the dog over your back and throw the treat. The dog should not touch your back as this will risk sticking in the final version of the exercise as well (unless of course, you want your dog to jump onto you before jumping off again). If the dog still doesn't jump over you, try to raise the jumping pole a little bit so it might be able to distinguish it from you. If the dog still doesn't jump, go back and do a few repetitions of the normal agility jump, and then have your helper help from the beginning next time you crouch down.

When the dog is starting to jump over your back, slowly try to raise your arms backwards over your back. This will help mark the area where the dog should jump just like the wings of the normal agility jump does. This way you can help ensure that the dog doesn't jump sideways over you.

When your dog is comfortable and consistent in jumping over your back, remove the jump pole and do a few repetitions without it. After that, you move away from the jumping equipment, crouch down as far as possible and try to do a few repetitions with only your body as the jumping target. Lift your arms up over your back to help guide your dog.

When it consistently jumps over your back without the agility jump equipment, you are ready to slowly stand up more and more. This has to be very slowly to ensure that your dog lands correctly and safely every time. At some point soon, you will be able to stand up as much as you want (to what is an acceptable height for your dog's size).

Main points:

- Teach your dog to jump over a normal agility jump
- Have it jump without you running with it
- Use distance rewarding
- Crouch under the jump pole with your head bend down (you can increase the height of the agility jump here slightly if you need to)
- Get your dog to jump over you – maybe have a helper
- Raise the jump-pole to get your dog to jump higher to prevent it from touching you in the jump
- Use your arms as guidance for your dog
- Remove the jump-pole and have your dog jump over you
- Move away from the agility jump and have the dog jump over you
- Slowly try to stand up more and more
- Ensure that the dog jumps far enough to properly stretch its legs to make sure that the dog lands safely every time

Challenge #2 – jumping through your arms

The first step of this challenge is the exact same step as the first one in the above challenge. So get out the agility jump equipment.

Now, instead of crouching under the jump-pole, you place yourself standing in the middle of the agility jump with your back towards the jump-pole. Then get your dog to first jump over the agility jump on one of your sides, and then move behind you from where it landed to jump over the pole again on the other side of you. Have your dog circle you like this while jumping a few times. Make sure, before you proceed, that you can do it entirely on verbal cue and don't rely on body language.

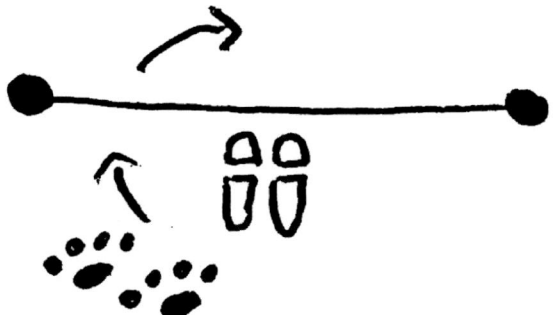

Figure 7 - Stand in the middle of the agility jump and have your dog jump over the agility jump on one of your sides.

Figure 8 - Once your dog lands on the other side of the jump behind you, have it jump back in front of you by jumping over the jump on the other side of you. This way it is jumping around you in a circle.

When you are able to do it smoothly on verbal cues only, or at least very discreet hand signals or body language, you are ready for the next step. Hold your hands and expand your arms as wide as possible. It is best to practise this in front of the mirror, so you can see how wide you spread your arms, as often people don't realise that they don't spread them wide enough and don't allow much space for the dog to jump through. So get it well into your muscle memory. When you can create a proper big wide circle with your arms, hold them down on one side of you, just above the jump pole, and ask your dog to jump through. Now switch your arms over to the other side of you to get your dog to jump through again. If your dog doesn't jump through, go back to the previous step and repeat that step more. Also remember to practise on holding your arms wide and creating a proper circle. If your dog still doesn't jump through when you return to this step, have a helper lure the dog through the first couple of times, or slowly practise holding your arms differently at the previous step. If your dog still doesn't seem to understand it yet, try to teach it to jump through a hula hoop first, then use the hula hoop next to you while standing in front of the agility jump. Then slowly move your arms along the hula hoop closer and closer together until you form a circle with your arms. This way you will be able to phase out the hula hoop!

When your dog jumps through both your arms smoothly and consistently, remove the jump-pole. Have your dog jump through your arms again.

When you can do this without problem, step away from the agility jump equipment and do a few repetitions there. Finally, your dog is able to jump through your arms!

Main points:

- Teach your dog to jump over an agility jump without you running along with it
- Use distance rewarding
- Place yourself in the middle of the agility jump with your back against the jump-pole
- Have your dog jump over the pole on one of your sides, then run to your other side and jump over the pole there as well
- Have your dog jump around you in a circle on verbal cues only
- Make big circles with your arms and place them on your side just above the jump-pole and ask the dog to jump through
- Do the same for your other side
- Remove the pole
- Step away from the agility jump

Challenge #3 - Fly left, fly right

Another variation of the above fly game can be asking your dog to jump over your stretched out arms instead of through circles you make with your arms. The first many steps are the exact same, but when your dog is able to jump around you consistently and smoothly, get down on your knees and place your legs underneath the agility jump. Then stretch out your arms and put them at the height of the agility jump pole. Simply get your dog to jump over, or have a helper to start you out.

Figure 9 - How you should position yourself in relation to the agility jump once you are ready to start having the dog jump over your arms.

Challenge #4 - Sideways backflip

Who wouldn't want to teach their dog a sideways backflip on a tree? It looks pretty cool! It can also be done on vertical walls - but this should only be done once the dog is super confident in this exercise - so not when the dog does it correctly 8 out of 10 times on a tree, but 10 out of 10 every day you try. Walls are more steeper, more slippery and therefore more difficult, and we do not want to surprise our dog in a negative way, so make sure that your dog really knows the trick before attempting this trick on walls!

The first thing you want to do is to either find a tree that is leaning considerably to one side, or has a wide bottom that you can use. You can also use a sturdy plate that you can adjust the steepness of if it has been properly secured so it won't move when the dog jumps onto it. Box mattresses are actually quite good for this.

Then start by putting your foot against the tree and stretch your leg. Simply have your dog jump over your leg a couple of times. Once you've done this successfully with your dog a few times, you can try to move a little closer to the tree while keeping your foot in the same place. This way your knee will start to bend slightly. You will now have to ask your dog to jump over your leg, but only the lower part of your leg (from the knee and down) so it comes closer to the tree. Once this has been repeated with many successes, move closer to the tree yet again. At some point, your dog will be so close to the tree that it will find it easier to jump over your leg, if it touches the tree and uses it to kick away from - praise a LOT for this, when the dog just slightly touches the tree in the beginning! Repeat this many times.

When your dog is good at touching the tree, you should add a verbal cue. This should not be the same cue as a normal jump, as this jump involves a vertical surface it has to touch, whereas normal jumps don't involve anything it should touch. Some say "salto", others say "flip". I call it "hop". You can try to phase out the use of your leg by gently kicking towards the tree instead of having your leg on the tree all the time. You can also try to give the dog a little more distance it can use to gather speed for jumping - in this case, try to see if you can run with it, and when you reach the tree, either just point towards it and say your desired cue, or gently kick towards it to help with the leg - just be sure that you do not accidentally kick your dog.

Main points:

- Find a leaning tree or a sturdy plate you can adjust the steepness of.
- Put your foot against the tree and ask your dog to jump over your leg.
- Slowly, decrease the distance between you and the tree by bending your knee and have your dog jump over the lower half of your leg.
- If the dog by accident touches the tree, praise it loads to really reinforce that NOW it did something really good!
- Introduce a verbal cue when the dog is consistent at touching the tree when jumping.

- Try to phase out the use of your leg by running with your dog, or removing your leg from the tree while the dog is jumping.

Extra tricks that are useful for dog parkour

I will here in this chapter go through some of the most essential and fun extra tricks that can be useful for dog parkour. Tricks can be used to make your dog parkour games different, more challenging, and more fun. If you are more interested in tricks you can find many, many more in my online training classes which can be found at Www.4pawscanineacademy.com

Slalom

Slalom games are especially great in cities where you might encounter loads of pillars or in parks with trees planted in straight lines. If you want to go pro with these games you should obtain an agility slalom with training arches or find a place where you can use one.

The training arches will help your dog to do the exercise correct from the beginning and thus prevent it from doing it wrong. With time, the dog will build up muscle memory for this exercise, and it will know how to correctly do the slalom, properly alternating between walking in the middle of two obstacles entering from the right and from the left.

When the dog has built up this muscle memory, you can try to remove some of the training arches and let your dog do the slalom. If it does it correctly, repeat with the same amount of arches for a couple of times. If it consistently continues to do the slalom correctly, you can gradually remove more and more training arches until you have none left. When your dog is able to do this you can then try to transfer this exercise onto other objects instead of the agility slalom.

If you want to be able to have your dog complete a whole series of slalom obstacles without you having to run with it, be sure to practise the agility slalom without you running with your dog as well.

Twist and Spin

Twists are pretty simple, easy to learn, great for the dog's motor skills and muscles but it also looks super cool!

For dog parkour they are mainly used as tricks on top of platforms but with a good imagination I'm sure you can come up with more uses for the twists in dog parkour.

Anyhow, when starting out trying to teach your dog a twist I have found that luring in the beginning gives the absolute best result. Simply have a treat in your hand and have the dog in front of you. With the treat, lure your dog in a big circle. To make it easier for yourself, make sure that you start with your dog standing close to you, as you will have to make the circle motion away from yourself. By having the dog close, it will be easier for you to make the whole circle without feeling that your arms are too short. When your dog has completed the whole circle, give it the treat and praise it. Remember to practise both sides! Just be aware, that dogs can be left-minded and right-minded just like people can be left- or right-handed. It might therefore be easier to do it in a certain direction. But if you do not practise both sides, you can end up with a dog that is not straight in its back and have uneven muscle mass. This is why you have to do both sides.

As soon as it becomes easier both for you and your dog to complete the full circle, you can begin to put in a verbal cue. Remember to choose different verbal cues for the different sides. A piece of advice when choosing verbal cues to different versions of the same trick is to choose cues that do not sound alike and do not start with the same sound. I used to have "twist" and "turn" for my first dog, but since he was so eager to please me, he didn't wait to listen for which of the two words I ended up saying. So he would simply offer one of the sides, but it wasn't always the right one. He simply heard the T-sound in the beginning and deduced that I were about to say either "twist" or "turn". Now with my new dog I have switched to "twist" and "spin" and he knows the difference and does it right every time.

When you have tried luring your dog while saying the verbal cue, you can begin to phase out your hand signal. You can try to lift up your arm a little bit more so it is not right in front of your dog's nose. You might also be able to switch out the treat with a toy instead to promote speed in the exercise. Gradually make your hand signal smaller and smaller and eventually try with a simple small motion with your finger. Remember to allow your dog to think for itself. When you get to the point where your hand signal is becoming smaller and you are not actually luring your dog around in a big circle, say the verbal cue and give your small signal – then wait for the dog to offer a behaviour. If your dog does not immediately do the Twist, simply wait. You might have to wait for what feels like 5 minutes (while it in reality is only 60 seconds) before your dog does something. If it then merely looks in the right direction or starts moving the right direction you have to praise it! If your dog really does not offer any behaviour at all, then help it with a bigger hand signal, but don't repeat your command again. If you repeat your command several times before the dog does the exercise, you might create a poor association between the command and the exercise, and your dog might learn to count how many times it is "allowed" to not do the exercise before you get properly irritated.

Wave

Waving with one of the two front paws is super cute and can also be used on top of platforms to increase the difficulty or to make the whole performance look even more amazing. It is, however, a super easy trick to teach and most dogs become super excited about this trick! Furthermore, it's a great warm up exercise as it both encourages focus on the handler as well as it gets the dog to stretch its leg and warm up its muscles.

In order to teach wave, it's easiest if you already know how to shake paw. But in case you haven't taught your dog to shake paw yet, I will first go through how to teach that as it is the fundamental exercise of the wave trick.

To teach your dog to shake paw you will need a treat in your hand. Show the treat to your dog and then close your hand. Now you just have to be patient and wait for your dog to paw at the hand in order to try and get the treat. If you feel like you have been waiting long and nothing is happening, then show the treat to your dog again and make it excited about the treat and quickly close your hand when it begins to show excitement. You should also remember to use high-value treats such as cheese, sausage or ham if your dog is generally a low-arousal dog. You can also try to move your hand around while it is closed to encourage the dog to interact with the closed hand. If the dog as much as lifts the paw off the ground or shifts its weight onto one side, then praise it for that and let it have the treat. Praising more often encourages the dog to keep the excitement high and learning will therefore be faster.

When your dog is able to shake paw I strongly suggest to put a verbal cue on it and practice many times with the verbal cue as well so the dog gets the association. The reason why I want you to give this a verbal cue before moving on to the wave is so you don't end up ruining your new exercise accidentally.

When you are ready to start the waving exercise, it's a good idea to start with a few normal "paws". This gives the dog the idea that we are working with the paws which then makes it easier to build on the exercise. Now it's important that you don't use the verbal cue for shaking paws as we are going to change the exercise. If you then use the cue you can end up ruining your "shake paw" trick. So without words, put your hand in front of you just as when you want your dog to shake paw and then just as the dog reaches out for your hand, you remove your hand right before the dog hits it. When you remove your hand your dog will at first be a little confused, so it is VERY important that you praise it for this. Otherwise, your dog might think that it did something wrong. Do this several times and remember to praise lots, even if the dog gets to a point where it only lifts its paw but doesn't try to hit your hand. This is still a good development from the normal paw as the exercise then already becomes more independent. When your dog lifts its paw from the ground every time, you can start to use a verbal cue to help the dog understand that it is in fact a different exercise.

If you enjoyed training these extra tricks, you can find many more tricks at 4-Paws Canine Academy's online training courses which can be found at www.4pawscanineacademy.com

Fitness for Dogs

Another way of using your dog parkour skills is by training dog fitness. Dog fitness is specifically designed for working with your dog's muscles and it's a great warm up for your dog as well. In this chapter I will shortly describe some of the fitness exercises for you that I find most relevant to dog parkour. Dog fitness might be called something different in your area, so keep your eyes and ears open if you would like to practise this regularly. It can also work as great inspiration for your dog parkour training and it might give you new ideas for ways you can use your environment.

Sit-Stand-Sit

This exercise is good for warming up your dog's hips and thighs as well as getting the elbows moving. You can either use a half-ball, a paw pad, a platform or yoga block. The purpose here is to start with your dog standing with its two front feet on the prop and maintaining this position. The goal is for the dog to maintain its front paws in the exact same position and only move the hind part of its body. If you are a true expert, try and aim for movement only in the thighs as when people are squatting.

When you start out, simply lure your dog onto the prop and praise with a couple of treats for standing with the two front paws on the prop. Release your dog with its release cue and let it seek back onto the prop for a couple of repetitions to ensure the dog knows that we are working with this prop. Do not hold back on treats - praise several times for simply standing in the right position and maintaining this.

Then try to ask your dog to sit and see what it does. If it keeps its paws on the prop, then praise loads! If it steps off the prop, you might need to work a little bit more with its front paws on the prop. You can also try to use a different kind of prop as this can sometimes have an influence on the way the dog behaves.

You can also try to lure or shape your dog into a sit. Try to lure it with a treat and position your hand above the dog's head. Slowly move your hand a little behind the dog's head or move it down towards the dog's head - all depending on how your dog reacts to your hand signals. If the dog bends a little or starts "tucking" its hind paws underneath its body, verbally praise your dog and wait to see if it offers more. You can also give the treat here, but be aware that this might cancel the behaviour so you will have to do this several times. It can however, the more you praise for each tiny step, also help promote confidence into getting the right behaviour, so the approach you take is entirely up to you and how your dog is. You can also simply wait for you dog to offer a new behaviour, and then hope to see it moving into a sit.

Repeat these changes in positions a couple of times to train the muscles in the thighs and around the hips. If this is for warm up, do not change too quickly between the positions as we want a gradual and slow warm up to begin with to prevent any strains. Do not continue this for too long either, as a dog's muscles can become sore just like ours and we don't want to over-train our dogs.

Balance

For this I would recommend using either a half-ball or a whole yoga ball that is secured to prevent it from rolling. Get your dog on top of this ball and have it stand with its weight evenly distributed - this is achieved when the dog or the ball is not shaking anymore. The dog uses its entire body for this so it is great for building up general muscle mass without a specific focus area.

To increase the difficulty and getting to get the dog moving to actively reobtain its balance, you can ask it to perform different tricks on top of the ball. Try to get your dog to twist on top of the ball. You might have to lure it in the beginning as it can feel weird in the beginning. Be sure to reinforce your dog all the way to the completed trick, to ensure you give your dog a positive experience. The more you train these kinds of things where you ask your dog to perform unusual behaviour in unusual situation, you will build your dog a stronger and stronger confidence and self-esteem along with a much better self-awareness with regard to its own skills and physical movements.

If your dog needs a bigger challenge, try to get it to sit pretty on top of the ball. This requires an amazing balance and awareness of its own body. Before attempting this, be sure that your dog knows the exercise on the ground beforehand. However, even though it knows this trick normally, you might find it useful to help your dog in the beginning by luring with a treat above its head. Remember, whenever you increase the difficulty of any trick with your dog, it might need a little extra help to ensure a success the first couple of times - and this is totally alright! This trick will strengthen the muscles in the dog's back immensely as it both uses them for sitting upright, but also for keeping its balance on the ball.

If you have a half-ball you can also flip it over so the round part of the ball is on the floor, and the flat part is looking upwards. Get your dog to do different things on the ball while it is able to tip around like this. This can be quite difficult, but it is a good way to practise balance, self-awareness and control of their bodies. Try and do different games such as I'm the King game or On Top of The World game.

Bows and push-ups

You can always use normal bows for warming up your dog's muscles, but if you want to take it a step further or stretch the dog's back and warm up the muscles in the front legs as well, you can use a prop to do a bow from. Don't use a prop that is too high, but a platform or yoga block is always a good option for this. You could potentially also use a half-ball. Your dog should start with its hind legs on the prop and stand with its front paws on the ground. Lure your dog into a bow by having a treat in your hand and placing your hand towards the dog chest and a little bit towards the ground. By doing this you help your dog stretch its back and use its muscles in its front legs.

● ● ●

If you want to make sure that your dog stretches its back properly, both bending the back in a U shape and bending it in an opposite U shape (more like an n shape or an arch), then you need to lure it again. The normal bow, the U bending, can be quite simple. The arch shape can be a little bit more tricky if you haven't practised it before - but don't be put off! This is good for your dog and isn't too difficult either. When you have your dog standing with its hind legs on the prop and its front legs on the ground, lure your dog with a treat between its front paws from underneath its body. You should aim to lure your dog's head down between its front legs, preferably looking towards its own navel. This way the dog bends its back like an arch.

All paws on

For this you would need 4 paw pads, one for each paw. This exercise is excellent to promote more body awareness in the dog, but also very useful for different stretches once your dog gets more experienced and is able to "glue" its paws to the pads.

You can start this exercise easy by asking your dog to put a paw on each pad. You might have trained the front paws with targets before, but you should also remember to train the hind paws. It is useful if you have a different cue for each paw.

If you haven't tried teaching your dog hind-paw targets before, simply place a paw pad in between the dog's front and hind legs. Try and lure your dog to move onto it with one of the hind paws and praise for this! Remember, the more you praise for behaviours that could potentially lead towards the desired behaviour, the faster you will get there, and the more confident your dog will be in the exercise in the end. When you are more easily able to lure your dog onto the target with its hind paw, you can begin to use a verbal cue to further enhance this behaviour and make it stick in the dog's brain. Soon it will have this behaviour integrated in its muscle memory too. You can then do this for all four paws if you want to.

If you don't feel like teaching the dog different cues for all the paws, you can also potentially lure your dog onto standing with a paw on each pad. Simply place the pads where your dog would normally put its paw - so with the same length between the pads as the dog is normally having between its paws. Then try to lure it with a treat onto the pads and praise as soon as it touches any one of them with any one of its paws.

When your dog's paws are properly "glued" onto the pads - meaning that it knows not to step off the pads before getting a release cue, no matter how much you are luring it, you can start to get it to stretch in different ways. You can either lure it to stretch for a treat in front of it and thereby stretching the back and its hind legs. You can also do the opposite and place a treat a little towards the dog chest to get it to lean backwards and thereby stretch its front legs. You can also use this position to stretch the dogs back by using U bending and arch bending.

If you need a bigger challenge for your dog, flip over the paw pads so they can wiggle and then get your dog to balance on top of them again. This can be quite difficult, so start with one where it should have both front paws. Then move onto using two, one for each front paw. You know your dog is in full control of its balance when it can stand entirely still on top of these without shaking or wiggling.

Stretch the entire body

For this you would need something tall such as a tree or a wall. The purpose is to get the dog to stretch its entire body by leaning up onto something vertical such as a tree or a wall. Your dog doesn't need to already know a cue for this, as this behaviour can usually be lured in the moment.

All you need is treats in your hands. You then simply clap a few times with your hand onto the obstacle you want your dog to stretch on and then hold your hand with a treat above the dog close against the obstacle. As soon as your dog offers to put one or two paws on the obstacle, praise it! In the beginning it doesn't matter if the dog actually stretches or not. Simply do this a couple of times to ensure that your dog knows we are working with placing the paws on something. Slowly, you can begin to require more and more stretching my simply withholding the treat. Just do not wait too long before praising if this is new to your dog. Make sure your dog experiences a success.

Assessment and Titles

Assessment and Titles

At 4-Paws Canine Academy it is also possible to win Dog Parkour Titles! The titles are not part of any competition against other dogs but are merely assessments of your own dog's performance and your teamwork together.

Go to www.4pawscanineacademy.com/dog-parkour to read more about obtaining a dog parkour title for your dog!

> At 4-Paws Canine Academy we value teamwork between a dog and its handler very highly! Assessments are therefore made with the demonstration of teamwork in mind.

The different 4-Paws Dog Parkour Titles

The First Leap (Novice) - This is your dog's very first Dog Parkour Title and requires demonstration of the most basic and fundamental exercises of dog parkour.

The Progressor (Intermediate) - This is the next level title your dog can achieve. Here the fundamental exercises will require more precision and independency, and there will be other exercises as well to challenge your dog.

The Hero (Advanced) - This is one of the more challenging and demanding titles your dog can achieve. Here your dog is required to demonstrate true understanding of the different exercises as well as great independence in its performance. The Hero Title also requires the exercises to be linked together in chains which have to be performed without interruptions in between the different exercises.

The Parkour King (Expert) - This title is similar to the previous title in terms of many of the exercises but it requires that at least half of the exercises are linked into a chain.

The Dog Parkour Champion - This is the highest title your dog can obtain and requires all the exercises to be linked into a single performance chain. At 4-Paws Canine Academy we value teamwork very highly, and you, as the handler, is therefore also required to be part of this performance in some way so the strength of your teamwork is also demonstrated.

For the complete set of rules, go to the dog parkour section on www.4pawscanineacademy.com

Using tires for dog parkour

How to use tires (and other ways to build your own props)

Old tires are AMAZING as dog parkour props and there really are no limits as to what you can do with them. I will, however, in this chapter attempt to spark your own imagination with quite a few examples of how you can use them as singular tires, or even how to build bigger obstacles with several tires.

Sit inside

You can start simple by just having your dog sit inside the middle of the tire. Then you can have your dog put its paws on the tire while maintaining the sit inside the tire. You can also improve this exercise by combining cool paw tricks with the original sit, such as shake paw, wave, or hiding its nose with one or two paws.

Play the King Game!

One of the more obvious choices is to play the King game with tires. Try to play it both with the dog standing inside the middle of the tire as well as outside the tire. You can even increase the difficulty by playing the Elephant game as well. This you can also do by either having the dog inside the middle of the tire, or standing on the outside of the tire.

Be on top of the world with the proper game!

Play the on-top-of-the-world game with your dog on top of the tire. You can increase the difficulty and fun level by teaching your dog to do different kinds of twists on top of the tire without stepping down from the tire. One version could be to let the dog walk around on top of the tire, simply following the tire around in the circle. Another version could be to have the dog stand with the front paws on one side of the hole in the middle, while standing with the hind paws on the other side of the hole in the middle, and then have your dog walk "sideways" round in a circle, so it keeps having two paws on one side of the hole and two paws on the other side of the hole.

Stretch out with the bum in the air game

You can also have your dog play the bum in the air game in different ways! You can do the simple versions by either have the front paws inside the hole in the middle with the hind paws on the tire itself, or you could have the dog put its front paws on the outside of the tire, while still standing with its hind paws on the tire. If this is too easy, you can always teach your dog to walk around the tire while maintaining the rules of the bum in the air game, either with the front paws inside the hole or with the front paws outside the tire.

Through games

Another super fun way you can use tires is to place them upright with something supporting them so they don't end up tipping over, and then use them just like agility tunnels. If you have several tires, you can even set them up in a row after each other to create a "tunnel course". You can also place them on a straight line next to each other, so the dog would do a zig-zag-ing motion between them, using the through games as part of a slalom.

Up-down-up-down game

In this simple game you can either place a few tires lying down next to each other in a straight line, or you can cover a whole square of the ground with several tires. The point is, that your dog should first stand with two front paws on the tire, while two back paws are on the ground. Then it proceeds on the tire course, and puts the two front paws down in the middle of the tire, while the back paws are on top of the tire. Again, your dog proceeds forward in the tire course, and puts its two front paws on top of the tire again, while the two back paws are in the whole in the middle of the tire. Then simply proceed and complete the full course like this with your dog. This is all about precision and requires you to walk slowly with your dog, so this is considered a good warm-up exercise as it stretches your dog's entire body and makes it use all its muscles. To get the most out of this exercise for warm-up purposes, make sure to pause in between each position to ensure that your dog's body properly stretches in this mode and is not just a part of its normal walking behaviour.

Military game or The Floor Is Lava

Place all the tires on the ground, forming a big square or rectangle as in a military obstacle course. You can use this in several different ways, which is only limited by your own imagination. But for now, you can simply use them as they do in the military - an obstacle course which simply has to be completed - either by jumping from hole to hole, or by running on top of the tires.

Sit-Stand-Sit game

This game is extremely simple but also incredibly useful for warming up muscles or building more muscle mass in the dogs. Start with your dog simply sitting down in front of the tire but with its two front paws on the tire. Then, while maintaining the position of its feet (especially the ones on top of the tire if it is just for the warm-up), the dog should try to stand up instead of sitting down. Once it has been standing for a few seconds, make it sit again while keeping it paws on the tire.

If you would prefer to build more muscle mass, then try to have your dog move from a sit to a stand to a sit without moving any of its legs, but simply using its thigh muscles to move.

The Time Game

A tricky game to play with tires is the Time Game. It is most definitely possible to play, but the tricky part is getting the dog to actually walk *around* the tire without touching it in any way, i.e. walking over the tire or on top of it. For the first couple of times playing this game, you can ensure your dog a success by putting up a fence closely around the tire. If possible, you can then later try to put the fence inside the tire and then gradually build towards removing the fence entirely. It is a fun game that really challenges your dog's knowledge about and confidence in its games.

Building your own props

If you are a bit of a handy(wo)man, you can also try and build your own props with a few tires and some extra material. Some of these props might be best for areas with lots of space, so check if you can get permission to put up these obstacle dog parkour props in either a dog park or at your outdoor dog training centre or club.

Slalom course and tunnel circles

You can attach tires to each other by joining them side-by-side. Depending on what you are planning to use the tires for, you can either line them up in a row and secure them to a strong frame (maybe made by wood), so you can use the tires as a slalom obstacle.

A different kind of structure you can build could include a circular "slalom" obstacle. To build this, you still join the tires together in the sides, but you place them in a big round circle, so you have a circle of

vertical standing tires. This you can use to train direction training with your dog when you direct your dog to a certain tire opening. This kind of training gives you amazing skills which can be transferred to agility purposes. It can also be used as an alternative way to do the slalom - remember, dog parkour is all about coming up with new ways you can use your environment and challenge your dog.

Balance obstacles

To make a prop especially for training your dog's balance and strengthen its self esteem you will need two plates of an approximate size of $1m^2$ along with three tires. Place one of the plates horizontally and fasten a tire on top of it. Make sure you have secured the tire at least 4 different places positioned equally around the tire so this bit does not move. Then you place another tire on top of the first one, but this one you only join in one or two places in the same side, so the tire can actually tilt on top of the other tire. Then you place the third tire on top and secures it to the tire below again using only two points close to each other, but placed somewhere else than with the tire below, so the tires feel a little unstable and you try to shake them a bit. Finally secure the last plate on top of the last tire to make a platform for the dog to sit or stand on. The plate should be properly secured with at least 4 points positioned equally around the tire.

When you get the dog on top of this, it might move a little bit, so be sure to support your dog and ready with lots of very high-value treats to reinforce your dog and potentially calm it down if it feels a little insecure. The whole structure will shake a little, if the dog does not position its balance evenly on the plate. You then have to teach your dog, to remain calm on top of this structure, and in doing so your dog will also practise its balancing skills and it builds up muscles in the entire body as well. When your dog is able to stand calmly on the prop with its weight distributed evenly on the plate, try to make it switch positions by asking it to sit. You can switch between easy positions like this to improve its balance and encourage build up of muscle mass. If you feel like a true challenge and your dog is confident about being on top of this prop, try to ask it to do more advanced tricks such as "sit pretty" with its front paws in the air.

Flying games

Get your dog to jump through the tires with a structure similar to the agility wheel prop. You can either make a frame and then secure the tire to each corner in the frame and thereby simply making an agility wheel, or you can make a bigger frame with space for several tires, either located next to each other or at slightly varying heights - just be careful you don't accidentally end up making them too tall! You can attach the tire to the top by using a rope, but be aware, that only securing it at the top will make the tire unstable and able to move quite easily if your dog should accidentally touch it when it jumps. This could be a safety hazard, so make sure to also secure it to the bottom somehow. For this you should also aim for using bigger tires so you do not risk your dog hitting its back on the tire when jumping through.

Buried tires

One last thing you could also do with your tires is to bury them halfway into the ground in a vertical position, so half of the tire is still above ground. This way you can use them for crawling exercises with your dog, or you can have your dog balance on top of the tires and walk from one tire to the other.

Final words

I sincerely hope that you have enjoyed reading my book and found inspiration for your own dog training journey with your dog.

I would like to invite you to e-mail me any questions that you might have regarding dog parkour or the book. You can find my e-mail address at 4-Paws Canine Academy's website.

Have fun in your continuous dog training journey.

Your success in dog training - and in particular dog parkour - is only limited by your own motivation and imagination.
-Anna Louise Kjaer

Acknowledgements

Heaton, W. H., Marr, K. C., Capurro, N. L., Goldstein, R. E., & Epstein, S. E. (1978). *Beneficial effect of physical training on blood flow to myocardium perfused by chronic collaterals in the exercising dog.* Circulation, 57(3), 575-581.

Helton, W. S. (2007). *Skill in expert dogs.* Journal of Experimental Psychology: Applied, 13(3), 171-178.

Miller, P. E., & Murphy, C. J. (1995). *Vision in dogs.* Journal-American Veterinary Medical Association, 207, 1623-1634.

Mitchell, Tom. (2018). *How to be a concept trainer.* London: First Stone Publishing

Murdock Jr, B. B. (1962). *The serial position effect of free recall.* Journal of experimental psychology, 64(5), 482.

Zink, C., & Van Dyke, J. B. (Eds.). (2018). *Canine sports medicine and rehabilitation.* John Wiley & Sons.

Made in the USA
Las Vegas, NV
10 November 2021